Robert Louis Stevenson's .... letter on Damien of
Molokai is one of the m................... f a
fellow human being e............................ EN
THE LEPER is a mag............................... life
the story of the heroic............................... end-
ary throughout the world.

The memory of Father Damien will surely endure as long
as men thrill to adventures of the spirit. For if ever a man
exemplified the human frailties and the great strength of mankind, it was Damien de Veuster. Humble, headstrong, patient
and kind, he lived his life against the background of the lush
tropical splendor of the South Sea Islands surrounded by the
hopelessness and degradation of the living dead. For many
years the unquenchable flame of his spirit gave new hope to
those who had been without hope. Then, one day, standing
before his alter, quietly and unostentatiously he began to ad-
dress his listeners, not as customarily, "My brethren", but
slowly and significantly, "We lepers".

John Farrow has revealed every facet of this amazing man's
being in a biography which is now a modern classic.
DAMIEN THE LEPER is so powerfully and so vividly written that the reader will feel, as did Hugh Walpole, that he
will "have Damien as a companion for the rest of his days."

JOHN FARROW

Damien the Leper

IMAGE BOOKS
A DIVISION OF
DOUBLEDAY & COMPANY, INC.
GARDEN CITY, NEW YORK

Image Books edition published October, 1954
by special arrangement with Sheed and Ward, Inc.

ISBN: 0-385-02198-7

CONTENTS

Excellentissimo et Reverendissimo in Christo Domino

JOANNI JOSEPHO CANTWELL, D.D.

Filiali cum Devotione

Hoc Opus Dedicatum Est

Very briefly I would like to say why I consider this book of Mr. Farrow's both true and beautiful. The world, in general, does not perhaps know the greatness of our Father Damien, and its main source of information has been the magnificent letter of Robert Louis Stevenson. For the first time, I think, the story has been told here in very simple terms and with the absolute stamp of truth upon it. The adventure of Father Damien is so romantic as to be almost unbelievable, unless there is at its heart a strong religious fire burning. The spiritual and physical drama of the subject makes melodrama easy and inviting. But Mr. Farrow is never melodramatic. He does not often build up the character of Father Damien from the outside but lets it gradually live of itself through the incidents, the letters, the criticisms of others until, when the book is finished, we feel that we have met, and even know, that strange, dogmatic, fanatical Saint of God.

Mr. Farrow is fortunate because he knows both the South Seas that are the background to the story and because his own religion helps him to understand, and believe in, the vision that Father Damien saw. He shrinks from no detail of the physical horrors of the scene. He contrasts them very cleverly—the beautiful background of earth, and sea, and sky. But at the center, perhaps, is this unfailing truth that "He who loses his soul for my sake and the Gospels wins a great victory."

I scarcely know how Mr. Farrow has been able to leave so vivid a picture of Father Damien in the reader's mind with so few words about him. I had not realized from Ste-

1

venson's letter the strange mixture of opposition that that stolidly irascible man presented. Now that I have read this book I feel that I have Damien as a companion for the rest of my days. This is an addition to one's spiritual experience, and I thank Mr. Farrow for it.

HUGH WALPOLE

PREFACE

It was on one of the more remote of the Society Islands that I had my first meeting with a leper. The island was particularly beautiful and I, enchanted with the sudden peace of the lagoon after a wretched passage in a small trading cutter, determined to stay there for a few days. A consultation was held with the amiable half-Chinese, half-Tahitian captain and the matter was arranged; he would proceed to the next island, pick up a cargo of copra, then return for me. Happily and innocently I went ashore. This was on a Monday and the cutter was to come back the following Thursday, but such are the ways of mariners in those pleasant waters that I was marooned for nearly three months before seeing his dingy craft again.

Excepting for a gendarme who lived in another village and who seemed to be a haughty individual, eyeing my shorts with pompous disfavor whenever, which was not often, we met, I was the only white man on the island, and as such was treated as a Personage. The natives were charming, and one hospitable family insisted I should stay with them; for it appeared they had a Bed, an article of furniture which in those regions denotes the owners as being persons of wealth, culture and initiative. My hosts were particularly proud of their bed and I did not blame them for it was truly a grand and huge affair, made of glittering brass and shining mother-of-pearl, ornamented with innumerable colored shells, and swathed in clouds of immaculate mosquito netting. In the evenings, when the time came for me to mount this luxurious couch, there would be something almost ritualistic in the way my solemn-eyed friends would gather to wave farewell as I, feeling rather like a Paladin making a ceremonious entrance to his tent, disappeared through the tall curtains. I slept soundly and with great comfort in it for two weeks; then, one morning, as I was carrying my fishing gear to the lagoon, I met the gendarme. "If you are interested to know," he said in the most casual of tones, "the bed you are sleeping in has been used by a leper."

My fishing plans were quickly forgotten and a frantic check-up revealed that the gendarme's information was correct. The former occupant of my bed, the son of my hosts, was a leper who, after being dispossessed in my favor, had been relegated to a hut of his own that stood behind the main house. To my further horror I learned we still shared the same meals and, presumably, the same dishes. I shall never forget that afternoon. I was angry and afraid. I stared at the glittering surfaces of the bed as though I might be able to detect germs. I scratched and scratched again before the agonizing irritations of countless imaginary itchings. I looked at my skin, half expecting to find the fatal white markings, and I scrubbed my body with strong disinfectants until the blood ran. I prayed for the return of the cutter so that I could get to Papeete and a doctor, but the horizon remained empty of sails and it seemed as though the Captain had forgotten my existence.

After a week or so, probably because of boredom and a pessimistic certainty of my fate, I began to visit the leper and we became friends. Many hours we passed together in front of his tree-shaded hut, talking in our mixed patois of French, Tahitian and English, or with me listening while he strummed a guitar and hummed the native songs. He was not more than twenty-five and seemed quite resigned to his awful affliction. As his story (and it is a tragic one) is not the one I wish to tell here I shall say no more concerning him; except that he had another friend, a Hawaiian ex-sailor, who told me he had been born at Molokai and that he had no fear of the disease because both his parents had been lepers.

This Hawaiian was a garrulous individual and full of stories, most of which were about the leper colony and the exploits of a heroic and, it seemed to me, highly fictional character called Kamiano. Such was the respect of my new friend for Kamiano that whenever he mentioned the name he would make a curious genuflection-like movement and throw a knowing look to the sky as though Kamiano were there and watching us. Tale after tale, inevitably punctuated with these innumerable bobbings of reverent salute, imbued me with a curiosity about the mighty Kamiano.

When I finally arrived back in Papeete I began to make inquiries. It was that gracious, noble and wise woman, the ex-Queen of Tahiti, who told me Kamiano was the native name for Damien. It was she who gave me a copy of Stevenson's letter, of which I had a vague remembrance, with instructions not to read it until I visited the leper hospital (at Papeete). I obeyed her. It was the beginning of an interest which took me to Belgium and back to the Pacific, and which is responsible for the following account of the Priest's life.

My gratitude is due to those who have helped me in the matter of research, among them Sister Damien Joseph of the Sacred Hearts Academy, Kaimuki, Honolulu, and the Princess Liliuokalani of Honolulu, the Rev. T. O'Toole of Los Angeles and Fr. Columba Moran of the Sacred Hearts Order. Also I owe thanks to the Honolulu Chamber of Commerce, the University of Hawaii library, the Huntington Memorial Library (California) and the libraries of the Royal Societies Club and Royal Geographical Society in London.

The year 1863 seemed to be the year for expeditions. English guns were barking at Maori spears on the shores of distant New Zealand. English troops, uncertain of recent victories, were marching in all directions in India. Foreign generals schemed in China. At Kogoshima Bay, on the coast of Japan, the bewildered and enraged followers of the Daimyo of Satsuma were receiving bloody salutations from the warships of white "barbarians." No region seemed too remote to escape the prowlings of military adventurers, and even the vast oceanic frontiers of America proved insufficient against the prevailing fashion of invasion.

The Monroe Doctrine was nearly forty years old but the United States was far too engrossed within her own boundaries—at least such was the opinion of Napoleon III and his advisers—to play the protector to less powerful neighbors. Civil War was dividing the great Republic. As slaves despaired and hoped, a Confederate General maneuvered on to Gettysburg. Further south, to the sharp music of trumpet and drum, the Standards of France were landed and once again were flaunted triumphantly on foreign soil. Despite demurrings from the Vatican, the too enthusiastic reports from the French Command in Mexico were eagerly received and read on the Adriatic terrace of lovely Miramar castle where a tall Archduke waited, nervously fingering newly grown side-whiskers as he gazed across the sea at the phantom of an Imperial Crown. By his side a young wife, dazzled by the same dangerous vision, wrote tremulous letters to Paris, and in that nervous capital alarmed citizens were beginning to wonder whether Bonaparte blood was to assert itself again, as maps were studied in the Tuileries.

In the same city, late one autumn night, while dynasts planned and troups embarked, another expedition, neither militant in aim nor large in size, was being considered in a drab building, unmistakably an ecclesiastical establishment, that squatted amid the shadows along the Rue Picpus. All the windows of the monastery (for that is what it was) save one, were darkened. From behind its uncurtained panes a cleric, in a scarlet-tinged mantle, stood watching the rain slash the gloom that obscured his favorite view of an outside world into which he rarely ventured. A rising wind provided fitting music for the wildness of the night and across the street familiar silhouettes were suggested rather than seen through the sleet.

The long, low-ceilinged room in which he stood was almost devoid of furniture, yet somehow it did not seem austere. Perhaps that was because of a coal fire smouldering in an old-fashioned grate or perhaps it was because of the hundreds of books stacked irregularly against walls which were washed white and completely bare except for a small wooden crucifix placed high and directly opposite the window where the priest kept his vigil. The furnishing of the room was completed by two chairs and a table.

Upon the table, among heaps of massed documents, was the one note of luxury in the room, a terrestrial globe, handsomely made, with a solid base of teak and silver and a sphere of lacquered parchment upon which the nations were stained in deep colors. Standing with the dignity of Georgian simplicity its richness shone well in the ruddy glow of the fire and the soft light of the one candle on the table. Engraven on the silver was the name of the priest and his rank. A distant branch of his family existed in Ireland and they, proud of a kinsman who was Superior General of an Order not yet a century old but already girdling the world with hard-working missionaries, had given him this gift on his election to the high office.

He turned from the window to the desk, reflecting there was much work to do before seeing his bed. Matters of administration were increasing in scope and detail, and of this he was actually glad; it was a sign that the Order was flourishing. Documents were piled high on the table. A petition from Peru. A list of farming implements needed for the mission in the Marquesas. A report to the Propaganda. A request for new vestments to be sent to the Gambier Islands. (The Order had been there for thirty years.) Voluminous correspondence with a shipping company in Germany, concerning a ship chartered to convey a contingent of missionaries to the Sandwich Islands.

Sitting down, he carefully selected a quill and began to write slowly, in a fine slanting hand, pausing for reflection between each phrase:

Advice To Be Read on Shipboard

To find the good in a thing at once is a sign of good taste. Some seek the good in life, others the ill. There is nothing that has no good in it. But many have such a scent that amidst a thousand excellences they fix upon a single defect as if they were scavengers of men's minds and hearts. So they draw up a balance sheet of defects which does more credit to their bad taste than to their intelligence. They lead a sad life, nourishing themselves on bitters and garbage. They have the luckier taste who amongst a thousand defects seize upon a single beauty that they may have hit upon by chance . . .

His hand lingered over the paper for a moment. From past experience he had found that young missionaries, newly ordained, full of the importance of their mission, were sometimes, in their zeal, overharsh to their charges. And intolerance was the last thing he wished.

The sound of a footstep made him look towards the door. Another cleric had entered, a stout, healthy individual with a broad, red face and a shrewd eye, now fixed on the Superior in a half whimsical, half despairing manner.

9

Dragging a huge silver watch from his soutane he said nothing, but dangled it reproachfully.

The other leaned back in his chair and smiled. *"Dies et nox"* he said, waving an expressive hand towards the desk. "But it has to be done, eh, Pierre?"

"Nothing will be done if you are forced to a sick-bed," grumbled the newcomer.

Although with no rank and, in fact, serving as the other's secretary, he spoke with the license of friendship. And, indeed, they were friends, old friends; and had been so since seminary days. Although the same age, both still in middle life, they were utterly unlike in every respect, appearance, temperament, even speech. The Superior was tall and thin, his features were aquiline and when he spoke it was with the clarity of Tours; whereas his friend's speech was unmistakably of a region close to Marseilles.

For a few moments they discussed ordinary business, then the conversation drifted on to other topics, but never far from their profession. A certain Cardinal Pecci was making a great name for himself with his masterly remonstrance to Victor Emmanuel on behalf of the Umbrian Bishops. Then there was the gratifying news from China that the Tientsin Treaty was being respected. Missionaries now had a fair chance of safety under the protection of an Imperial Army recently re-organized by a young English soldier named Gordon, who later was to die at Khartoum.

As the Superior conjectured on the possibilities of sending a mission to Tibet, Father Pierre's roving eye lighted upon the unfinished manuscript on the desk. It reminded him of an affair of discipline within the Order, something nearer to his practical mind than the vague possibilities of future competitions with Lamas. From the Picpus House at Louvain a young monk still in minor orders had, without the consent or even knowledge of his immediate superiors, written directly to the Superior General, begging permission to be one of the party leaving for the far away islands. Writing with fiery zeal and in faulty Latin, the supplicant had explained that he wished to fill the place made vacant by the sudden illness of his elder brother, an ordained priest. Father Pierre frowned as his mind dwelt on the rashness of this misguided youth. He should be punished, and quickly; for it would be a fine state of affairs if every student acted as though he had the privilege of communicating directly with the Superior General whenever the urge or desire moved him. The good secretary voiced his indignation but was met with indulgence.

"Surely such a wish to serve can be no great crime," urged the other. "Admittedly he is impatient, but such impetuosity can be excused by his years, or rather his lack of them."

" 'Hurry is a failing of fools,' " quoted Father Pierre heavily.

"On the other hand," persisted the Superior, "wise men often fail from procrastination. Celerity is the mother of good fortune and he has done much who leaves nothing over till tomorrow. *Festina lente* is a royal motto, as our young friend probably has heard."

Seeing that there was nothing to be gained from further discussion, Father Pierre merely raised his frame in a shrug that showed his disapproval of any contemplated leniency, then in expressive pantomime he once again dragged out the silver watch and eyed it meaningly. The hint was not lost upon his companion and as a sign of surrender the Superior arose, picked up the candle and walked towards the door.

As their footsteps echoed down the long corridor, he suddenly spoke, a twinkle in his eyes although his voice was stern.

"Pierre, you are right. The young man at Louvain should be, and will be, punished for his effrontery. To his Superior you will communicate the penalty for his transgression of discipline. He is sentenced to exile, banished to a life of servitude, loneliness and hard labor. In short, we will grant him the favor for which he so rashly pleaded. He may take his brother's place on the expedition."

With a dour face Father Pierre made a memorandum in the notebook he always carried. In a large and round lettering he wrote words that were to leave an echo, not only in the history of the Order, but in the story of civilization:

"For the Sandwich Islands—Damien de Veuster"

CHAPTER I

Some twenty-three years before the foregoing event took place, or, to be exact, on January third 1840, a midwife in the hamlet of Tremeloo in Belgium was hurriedly summoned to the home of François de Veuster. And as blankets were being warmed, neighbors came to congratulate the yeoman whose wife, Catherine, had just given birth to their sixth child, a son.

Among these good people was the most traveled man of the community, a ruddy-faced, hearty-voiced old soldier and kinsman of the de Veusters, who came booming into the kitchen of the farm house jovially roaring inquiries as to the sex of the new-born infant, a circumstance in which he had great interest and upon which he had wagered in favor of a male. Furthermore, he had promised to act, in the latter event, as godparent. If it had been a daughter the honor would have been refused, for, as he solemnly affirmed, distorting his saber-marked face with a tremendous wink at the feminine company present, the spiritual guidance of a female was entirely too much for an old soldier to undertake. Later, while sipping the congratulatory toast, he announced that the name of his charge would be Joseph, after the head of the Holy Family, his own Patron who had saved his life no less than four times. This last statement was the signal for chairs to be drawn around the fire and, while the old man told tales of war in foreign lands, the newly-named Joseph slumbered peacefully upstairs. And Joseph he remained until twenty years later when, on entering the religious life, he assumed in uncon-

13

scious prophecy the name of Damien, after the Saint and physician of that name.

A few weeks later the nearby church was the scene of the christening. To the font came the parents, awkward in the stiffness of their Sunday clothes; the brothers and sisters of the infant, round-eyed and wondering; a few friends and, of course, the noisy godfather who had donned a faded uniform for the occasion. The godmother was the youngster's maternal grandmother, a stern-faced matriarch who hushed her co-sponsor to a silence that was broken only by the necessary responses as the Curé performed his offices. They were pious people and silent prayers were offered as the child officially received its name and entry into the Church. Then the mother dutifully knelt at the communion rail and was "churched." While this rite was being enacted, the godparents fondled their charge, quite proud of the fact that he had made no commotion during the ritual. As they watched, the tiny clutched fist was lifted in a vague gesture that was sufficient to be thought an omen. The grandmother, convinced that the infant had made the sign of the cross, prophesied that he would grow to be a priest, but the veteran shook his head firmly and declared in his loud parade-ground voice:

"It was a salute! Who should know a military gesture better than I? He will grow to be a soldier and like his godpapa have adventures in foreign lands!"

The years proved that the grandmother had foretold the future correctly. But the veteran was not wrong either; for his godson was to visit distant lands and, although he carried no sword, was to have adventures amidst horrors that the old soldier would not have deemed possible.

Six years passed and Joseph was at the age when observation grows into fixed memories. With gratitude for his own good fortune, he munched his bread and cheese and with awe listened to his mother tell of a faraway land called Ireland where that year thousands of children were dying from

14

famine caused by the failure of the potato crop. It was about this time that his godfather, whom he now called Uncle, took him on an unforgettable first trip away from the village. On a market wagon they rattled to Malines. There the impressionable child saw the glories of a cathedral at its most impressive moment. A Pope had died and with all liturgical magnificence a Requiem High Mass was being sung for the repose of the soul of Gregory XVI. The Primate of the country was officiating; censers were being swung and as bishops and princes bent their knees, a rosary was fervently clutched in a small, grimy fist and the boy thrilled as he realized his prayers were ascending with those of such exalted company.

With the memory of this experience strong upon him, the boy sat silent and still, as the wagon rolled back to Tremeloo and the old man garrulously pointed out the sights of the countryside. Not that there were any great differences from the land surrounding their own village, excepting perhaps an occasional older church or taller windmill. The landscape stretched in flat expanses as far as the eye could reach, yet there was no monotony because of the patchwork of fields, continually changing in size and colors ranging from a rich green to an earth-brown.

If ever a region symbolized peace, it was this. No movement disturbed the serenity save the slow twist of a windmill on the horizon or perhaps a plowman furrowing the fields. No noise broke the quiet except those rural sounds that were a part of the general tranquillity: the deep-toned music of bells, the gurgling protest of a brook harnessed by the miller's wheel. Bordered by tall trees, the winding road was dotted by shrines, and always the sacred images were carefully kept and attended with offerings of freshly-cut flowers.

They were a pious people, the inhabitants of this calm region. Each village, amidst the clustered red-roofed dwellings, had its own picturesque spire reaching to the sky. In every hamlet the priest was the respected counselor and father to all. For centuries existence had continued thus, a simple pattern of life that made for contentment. Each man was satisfied with his lot: tilling the soil left to him by his fathers and to be left by him in turn to his sons. Each man observing the laws of his God and his fellow-men without rancor or envy, a practical example of happiness reached through Christian philosophy and teachings. If ever a man was born with a worthy reason for home-sickness in his later years, that man was Damien de Veuster who, with a childhood spent in this background of peace and beauty, calmness and safety, voluntarily sacrificed it all to serve among the horror of a settlement that no pen has ever yet been able, fitly, to describe.

The boy's first lessons in conventional education were received from his mother. There were few books in the farmhouse, and those there were had been in the family for generations. Written in ancient Flemish, they were mostly of a religious theme; because of its graphic wood-cuts the most popular with the family was a huge tome entitled "The Lives of the Saints." Every day in the late afternoon the three youngest children, two boys and a girl, Auguste, Pauline and Joseph, would congregate with their mother in the kitchen. It was their favorite time of the day; the father and older children were still in the fields and they had their mother, with the day's duties finished, to themselves.

The kitchen was a large, cheerful room, hung with polished copper pots and pans and with an open fire blazing beneath the iron spits. Auguste, with the dignity of an older brother, would stir the fire, a sweet biscuit would be issued to each, then the three would sit by their mother's feet as she delved into the volume and read of heroic deeds in the ancient days.

These were the stories that colored their childhood and, apart from a few local legends, were practically the only ones that they ever heard. It is no wonder, then, that even their games became flavored with a tinge of the ancient histories. While children in other lands and other homes played at Indians and soldiers and stormed nursery forts, these three young Flemings were the victims of a Roman mob, each one braving a roaring lion or a snarling centurion and each one taking reluctant turns at impersonating the same villainous characters. The farm garden became the Holy Land and the glories of the Crusades were relived. Bold knights battled savage Saracens among the cabbages until the uprooting of those vegetables would bring a scandalized roar from Papa de Veuster, and then friend and foe alike would scuttle back to the security of the kitchen. The woodcuts of the big volume would be pored over and the pictures of Saint's experiencing varieties of ferocious deaths would kindle the young imaginations; and, as the sparks flew from the kitchen fire, the minds of the children would paint vividly the agonies and fortitude of the early Christians at the stake. Doubtless these early impressions of faith and martyrdom helped to direct their own lives when in later years all three entered the service of the Church.

It must not be assumed that those children showed any especially holy qualities or were different in conduct from any other youngsters of their age. On the contrary, out of the one hundred or so children in the village, young Joseph was held to be not only one of the most daring in matters of youthful adventure but one of the most mischievous and obstinate. The favorite pastime of the village lads was to jump on the rear of passing wagons while a confederate or two would hurl a pebble at the horse which, when so startled, would immediately break into a wild gallop. Thus, for a few moments, hanging precariously, the heroes at the back of the wagon would enjoy a perilous, jolting ride until the wagon man, getting his horse under control, would dash at them in fury. This charming sport with its double dangers had the added spice of being forbidden by parents, but so wary and vigilant did the wagon men become that eventually only a few boys would attempt to essay the risk.

Among those adventurous characters was Joseph, much to the glee of his martial-minded godpapa, whose sympathies were entirely on the side of the miscreants and who, sad to relate, secretly encouraged them to the extent of offering a sweet as a reward for the most desperate sallies. Basking in the admiration of his fellows, Joseph, like many a hero before him, grew daring to a point of foolhardiness, until one unfortunate day he had the ill luck to fall in with an apparently slumbering driver of a wagon that slowly rattled through the village, presenting a tempting sight to the youngsters. Joseph jumped to the position of honor, the stone was thrown by his assistants, but the horse did not gallop, for the canny wagon man instead of being asleep was very much on the alert and had reined in his steed the moment the missile was hurled, and simultaneously numerous sympathizers of his emerged from hiding places to surround a dismayed Joseph. The boy managed to escape but not before receiving several hearty cuffs and a stinging cut from the wagon man's whip.

That evening Joseph did not appear for the meal hour and as the evening progressed he still was absent. His anxious parents started a search, but it was the godfather who finally found him *inside* the Communion rail of the village church, kneeling, apparently absorbed in prayer but nevertheless with an anxious eye on the door. The boy had remembered how, in ancient times, criminals could seek and receive immunity from their crimes as long as they remained near the sanctity of the altar. He refused to budge until he too received a promise of complete immunity. His parents arrived and before the eyes of the amused old soldier they tried to cajole the culprit away from the altar. They, too, realized they were in a sacred place where force could not be used. On bended knees and in hushed voices his mother pleaded and his father threatened, but Joseph remained firm. Eventually the promise was given in a hoarse whisper by his outraged father, and once again the de Veuster family was complete. Unfortunately records do not show how well that stern parent, François de Veuster, who was never known to spare the rod or spoil the child, kept his promise.

Another story is told of how the boy, after hearing a stirring sermon on the virtues of Charity, was accosted in the village street by a tramp who swore that no food had touched his lips for three days. Bidding him wait, the sympathetic youngster rushed to the de Veuster kitchen where by chance nobody was in sight to prevent him taking a large ham that had been carefully prepared by his mother for the family's midday meal. Not only did he give the mendicant the entire ham but also the dish in which it had been cooked. It is almost unnecessary to relate that there was once again a painful interview between father and son when the hungry farmer discovered the lad's practical application of the day's sermon.

Like other boys his life went on with its normal measure of hopes and joys, disappointments and sorrows. The only trait that seems to have differentiated him from his fellows in any way was a genuine liking for solitude, an inclination which became more pronounced as he grew older. Even in his earliest years (unlike his brothers who abhorred the chore) he found it no hardship to take his turn of tending the small flock of sheep possessed by the family. The meadows upon which the sheep grazed were by the banks of the small river Laak which flowed near the village. There, stretched out on the thick grass, the young shepherd would watch the river drift past. The gentle music of running water is a well known inspiration for the peace that leads to serious reflection. It was here, no doubt, he developed some of the self-containedness which led to the reticence that in later years was to bring accusations of taciturnity and surliness. The principle taught on his father's farm was that what must be done need not be said, and as Joseph grew older he seemed to learn the wisdom of using words sparingly. His father was fond of quoting the words of a wise old Jesuit: "Words bring familiarity and familiarity is never desirable; with superiors because it is dangerous, with inferiors because it is unbecoming."

His reticence became the seal of his capacity and by the time early adolescence was reached he had exhausted the resources of the small school at the nearby village of Werchter. Along with the elementary learning he had acquired at this institution, he had also gotten the nickname "Silent Joseph." But it must not be imagined that he was a recluse in any unhealthy sense of the word. The fact of his minding his own business did not prevent him from excelling in the games and interests of his fellows. Ice skating was the favorite sport of the countryside and when he became the local champion his own village was highly elated at possessing such a celebrity.

So when, wearing the mantle of this popularity, Joseph appeared at the door of the local smithy and cast an acquisitive and longing eye at the anvil, the good-natured smith, who was the hero of all the village lads, invited him to try his strength on the hot metal. The man and the boy became fast friends and every available minute Joseph had to spare he spent learning a few tricks from his crony's trade. As a side-line the smith took care of the village cemetery, adjoining the church; a work which included the digging of graves. Sometimes the boy assisted in the gloomy task, thereby, unknowingly, gaining experience that was to serve him well in the future.

The pleasant days drifted by and his father began to consider his future. The older children, like the generations before them, were to remain on and work the farm. Auguste, as did Pauline, showed signs of having a vocation for the life of a Religious, and to this the devout parents had no objections. At that time, in a rural community like Tremeloo, patriarchal authority was unquestioned. In matters of family discipline the father was supreme and his word was law. The de Veuster family was no exception to the prevailing custom, so when the head of the family, in view of the changing times, decided that his youngest son should be a merchant nobody even dreamed of saying nay, least of all Joseph. The elder de Veuster saw that a commercial career demanded a higher education and a more extensive knowledge of the world than Tremeloo could give his son, so he went for counsel to his friend, the village priest. After a lengthy conference it was resolved that the lad should be sent to an academy at Braine-le-Compt in the Province of Hainault. The chief object of his studies was to be French, for as yet he could only speak his mother tongue of Flemish, a provincial language confined to limited boundaries.

The Kingdom of the Belgians, though happily united geographically, is distinctly divided in the racial sense. The northerners are called Flemings, the southerners Walloons. Although of the same origin and although they have shared almost two thousand years of common history, they still speak different languages (Flemish and French). Between them exist rivalries nearly comparable, although perhaps not as violent, to those unfortunate feuds between northern and southern Irishmen.

The first few months at a Walloon school must have been none too pleasant to the young Fleming. Although utterly miserable at his first separation from home and not speaking a word of French he stoically went about his business, while his colleagues, with that cruel relish of persecution so familiar to schoolboys, baited him unmercifully. Not for long, however, did the hazing endure. Many hours spent with his friend the blacksmith had given Joseph muscles and a strength beyond his age, and he was quick to retaliate with a courage and fury that quickly gained him immunity and respect along the Academy halls. Making no complaints and with true filial regard he soon wrote reassuringly back to Tremeloo:

"It is with great pleasure that I take up my pen to write

you a short letter for the first time. By now I am quite accustomed to this place. I talk to the Walloons a little. I know my work, my lessons, my companions, and my bed. Everything in the house is clean and comfortable; our table is something like the one at the annual fair, and the beer is very good. Any Walloon that laughs at me I hit with a ruler. Our master is a Walloon but he is very good and learned; he gives me lessons in private. The first day I was a little shy, and I didn't like to ask for anything, though I had neither books, pens, paper, or anything I wanted. Afterwards I asked M. Derne, our master, for these things and he obliged. On Sunday we went for a walk. I walked with a Walloon, and asked the name of everything I saw. . . ."

With laborious diligence he continued to ask the name of everything until gradually he became fluent in the French tongue. The school terms slipped by and his sense of appreciation, a rare emotion in youth, increased. Realizing that college fees were a severe drain to a farmer's purse he wrote again:

"It is to you, my dear parents, that I owe the education which I am receiving and which will be useful to me all my life. I do not know how I can ever prove, as I ought, my gratitude to you for all the benefits you have conferred upon me from my earliest years."

Most of his schoolmates, besides being Walloons, were the sons of merchants and came from towns; and these differences of environment served to develop in him the tendency already shown in his childhood of relying upon his own company. The few hours of freedom from studies were spent alone, taking long walks into the country. He enjoyed no close friendships, and his sole confidences were made by letter to his brother who was serving his novitiate with the Picpus Fathers in Paris. Auguste, who by now had assumed the name of Pamphile, seemed happy in the monastic life and his letters showed such a contentment that Joseph read them with a touch of envy. For try as he could, it was impossible for him to feel any such enthusiasm for his own contemplated career. But filial obedience and gratitude to his hard-working parents made him continue to work at his studies with unrelenting vigor and the fruits of these labors in the form of official reports of satisfactory scholastic progress were received with great joy by his father. Belgium, at that time under the astute guidance of her monarch, Leopold I, was rapidly developing her international trade. Commerce was flourishing. Fortunes were being made in the towns. The Flemish farmer, de Veuster, was happy in the thought that he had guided his son's talents on the right path for a prosperous career.

But Joseph, tramping his lonely way along country roads, was beginning to grasp the full significance of how much the religious life appealed to him. Irresistibly he felt himself drawn towards the cloister. The final stimulus came when he attended his first Mission, conducted by the Redemptorist Fathers in their beautiful church at Braine-le-Compt. The messages of the sermons went straight to his heart, and not to his alone, for the church was crowded with enthusiastic congregations. As he listened to the exhortations, as he gazed at the mysteries of the altar, as he heard the impassioned chanting, and as his mind and being drank in all the beauties of the ritual, a great light of understanding seemed to descend upon him, clearing the perplexities of his soul. He realized with a sudden clearness that for him there could be only one career, not one of worldly wealth, but of poverty, humility and obedience; a career, the vicissitudes of which would be only known to Him who alone chooses his Apostles.

That night he remained awake, praying, seeking divine aid and guidance. The morrow was to bring the disagreeable duty of informing his parents of his decision and he knew well how bitterly disappointed his father would be. What made the task doubly hard was the knowledge that the hard-earned monies already expended on his commercial education had been raised only by dint of great sacrifice on the part of the frugal farmer and the rest of the family. Nevertheless his path was clear and had to be followed. In the morning he began the letter, first mentioning his sister who had taken the veil.

"What happiness is hers! She has made sure of the most difficult thing which we have to perform in this life . . . I hope my turn will come to choose the path I ought to tread. Would it not be possible for me to follow my brother Pamphile? . . ."

The abrupt request came as a shock and a complete surprise to his parents. It had become their habit in the evenings spent by the fireside to indulge, as parents will, in fond ambitious fancyings for their younger son's future; his letter arrived to destroy these hopes, to make seem for naught all the sacrifices that had been endured for him. The father's first reaction was to pen an angry reply, but the calmer judgment of his wife prevailed upon him to talk it over first with their old friend and adviser, the Curé.

That wise man listened to their tale, read Joseph's letter, and then wrote a confidential letter of inquiry to an acquaintance of his who served as an instructor at the school. The answer came quickly, telling of the boy's fervent attendance at the Mission and his deep and mounting interest in matters of religion. The priest then explained to the anxious parents that if their son actually was inspired with a genuine desire to enter the religious state, they should be the last to hinder or place obstacles in his way; but there was the possibility that his emotions, although sincere, might very well be only a temporary phase induced in an impressionable young mind by the eloquence of the Mission services. Time would tell. He advised the father to write a mild letter of doubt and surprise, rather than of disapproval, reasoning cleverly that to youth obstacles only serve to increase determination; if there were no opposition shown, no barriers of difficulty to be surmounted, the boy would be able more clearly and honestly to follow the dictates of his own conscience.

It immediately became evident that it was no temporary state of fervor that Joseph was experiencing. Few causes have been pleaded with such persistency; the months passed, and letters showing a respectful deference to his father's wishes but nevertheless filled with resolution flowed in a steady stream from the school to Tremeloo.

About this time his brother was transferred from Paris to the Picpus establishment at Louvain; a happening in itself of no importance yet serving to change completely the drift of Joseph's life. Not only was he determined to enter the service of the Church but so strong was his zeal that he had made up his mind to become a Trappist—a member of the most severe and austere of monastic orders whose vows are of perpetual silence, hard manual labor, and continual prayer. By letter he communicated this intention to Pamphile who, with brotherly sympathy and understanding and a great deal of wisdom, wrote back inviting him to come to Louvain. Joseph accepted with alacrity, and the second week of December (1858) finds him visiting, for the first time, a monastic institution. Pamphile with the pardonable pride of a young member took him around the house and explained the history and aims of the Order which had been founded by the French priest, Father Coudrin, at the beginning of the nineteenth century.

Their full title was and is the "Congregation of the Sacred Hearts of Jesus and Mary and of the Perpetual Adoration of the Blessed Sacrament of the Altar." But they have a more familiar name, the Picpus Fathers, derived from the street in Paris where Father Coudrin established his headquarters in 1805. The four stages of the life of Jesus Christ serve as inspiration for their aims. The education of children and training of aspirants to the priesthood is based on His infancy; His hidden life is symbolized by exercises of adoration; His public life by preaching and missionary work; and His crucified life by works of mortification.

Pamphile's enthusiasm for his Order was communicated to Joseph and, abandoning the idea of becoming a Trappist, the younger brother's ambition shifted in the direction of the Order of the Sacred Hearts. As there was still the matter of receiving his father's consent the brothers put their heads together and evolved a plan. On that day of the year when family feelings are particularly precious and dear, Joseph wrote home:

"I cannot hesitate to write to you on this grand Christmas Day, for this great feast has brought me to quit the world and embrace the religious state. His command to obey our parents does not apply only to childhood. Therefore, my dear parents, I implore you again for your consent; for without it I cannot venture to enter on this career . . . Auguste (Father Pamphile) writes to tell me that it will be possible for me to be admitted to his Congregation as a Choir-brother but that I should not fail to speak to the Superior at the New Year, and begin my novitiate a little later. Hoping for this great happiness, I sign myself, your obedient son. . . ."

After this letter his parents wisely made no attempt to stem the current of his wishes although the stubborn old farmer never, in actual words, gave consent to Joseph's entering the priesthood. However, about a week after the receipt of the letter, Monsieur de Veuster donned his Sunday clothes, left the farm in the care of his wife and children and set off for the school. It was Joseph's birthday and, surprised as the boy was at his father's unheralded appearance, he was still further astonished when the old man told him that, as he had a matter of business to arrange in Louvain, Joseph might as well accompany him into the town and spend a few hours with his brother at the monastery.

On the way the boy impetuously broached the subject so

dear to his heart, but Monsieur de Veuster gruffly declared that he did not wish to be bothered with such problems at the moment, his mind being occupied with the business that he had to conduct in Louvain. Like his son he was a man of few words. Never was he to make any confidences or give any explanations of what was to happen that day; but it seems almost sure that the genesis of that which occurred was conceived by him rather than by Joseph or Pamphile. Arriving at the Picpus house, he deposited the excited young man and abruptly told him that he was free to follow his own devices for the rest of the day and to take dinner with his brother but to be ready to leave in the early evening for the return trip. Left in the place that was so much a part of his ambitions and enthusiasms, Joseph was aware that the moment had come for his entrance into the service of the Church. After praying in the chapel he persuaded his brother to conduct him to the Superior, who seems to have been both kind and discerning.

At that age, his nineteenth birthday, Joseph was a young man exceptionally good to look upon. Along with the strength and healthy physique so necessary for a missionary's work, he had dark curly hair and a frank, handsome face, a face destined to be cruelly ravaged by the worst disease known to men, but at that time glowing with hope and youthful ardor.

After a short interview, the Superior, convinced that the youth's emotions were genuine and not merely transient, informed him that he could consider his future home to be with the Picpus Fathers. When François de Veuster arrived at the gates of the monastery to be confronted with his son's farewell, it is recorded that he showed no surprise, merely saying as though to himself in a resigned voice, "It is God's will."

Within the walls of the monastery the young student threw himself into the work of preparation with his habitual ardor, with too much ardor it might seem; a few nights after his admittance Pamphile, who shared a room with him, was awakened by the noise of uneasy stirrings and opening his astonished eyes he discovered his younger brother trying to sleep on the hard, bare boards of the cold floor. A spirit of self-mortification and a sense of penance had made the boy spurn the meager luxury of the monastery cot. Practices such as these were strictly frowned upon by the Order, so Pamphile routed him from the rigors of his penitential sleeping-place and ordered him back to the cot.

His training for a commercial career proved to be a drawback in the new life, for he had no knowledge of the classical languages. Therefore the authorities according to the rules of the Order had to place him among the Lay Brothers, with no hope of ever becoming an ordained priest. Joseph, whose sole ambition was to be of service, cared little about the rank or manner in which he achieved it; however menial or disagreeable the work set before him, he accepted and executed it as a part of that service.

The Fathers were building a larger chapel. He was ordered to assist the workmen in digging the foundation pits and carrying bricks. In clearing the ground for the new edifice it was necessary to tear down a tall mast-like chimney which, when the surrounding walls had been removed, swayed gently but ominously at the slightest provocation. The removal of this dangerous stack became an engineering problem. Because of the proximity of nearby buildings dynamite could not be resorted to and, not without reason, the sensible workmen refused even to venture within the danger zone. It was Joseph who finally scaled the tottering masonry, and beginning at the top, while all held their breath, calmly proceeded to remove brick after brick.

During the brief hours allowed for recreation Pamphile began to initiate him into the mysteries of Latin grammar. With his usual tenacity Joseph applied himself diligently to this new pastime. Morning, noon and night the echoes of conjugations could be heard in their room. It was to mean a great deal, this new familiarity with the noblest of all languages; there was now no reason, scholastically, why he should not be allowed to enter the ranks of those studying for the priesthood. Hence his superiors, beginning to realize the material they had in him, took some special pains to remedy his academic deficiencies. Scholarship never came easily to him. He was of the plodding type rather than the brilliant pupil, but with the goal of ordination now before him he displayed, at each stage of his ecclesiastical training, a stubborn determination to master thoroughly whatever branch of sacred or profane science was set before him.

The time arrived when he was to lay aside his baptismal name and adopt, as was the custom of the Order, a new one. Nobody seems to know why his fancy alighted on the name, Damien. Certainly, in view of his own life in the years to come, he could not have chosen a more appropriate patron than the brave physician of Cilicia who, after a life spent in the service of others, accepted, with his brother, the death of a martyr at the dawn of the fourth century.

In his ecclesiastical training there were long periods of self discipline. There were times when he was desperately unhappy because of a side of his nature which, although human, would have to be conquered if he were to become a worthy priest. He was prone to sudden flarings of anger, tempestuous outbursts, that were followed inevitably and quickly by the tortures of remorse. Everybody concerned, and anybody even who had been a witness to the incident, would receive apologies and in every way he would try to make amends. On his desk were engraved the words: *Silence, Recollection* and *Prayer.* With this motto continually before his eyes he remained at Louvain until the autumn of the next year when he was transferred to the Novitiate at Issy, near Paris. There, while October rain was falling, he took the three vows of poverty, chastity and obedience as a Brother of the Order in whose service he was determined to live and die.

Paris did not seem to awe the young Fleming. Of course

he had no opportunity to see many of the things that have made that city famous, but in the spring he did see the citizens cavorting at his favorite sport and, as an ex-champion, and with some disdain he wrote home:

"Today I believe we are going skating. I must ask Gerard to lend me his skates, because they don't know how to skate here. . . ."

The death of his grandmother occurred at this time and affected him deeply. She had been a good woman and had been exceedingly kind to him. This was the first occasion the Grim Reaper had struck close. He records that when told the unwelcome news, he turned pale and was forced to leave the refectory and seek the solitude of the chapel. In a letter of solace written to his parents he shows a philosophy and an acceptance of death strange in one of his youth. He urges them not to grieve:

"We must all die . . . So let us begin from this very day to prepare for a happy death. Let us not lose a moment of the little time we have still to live . . ."

The gay metropolis was gayer than ever that spring. Fashionable crowds thronged the newly-paved streets by day and crowded the gas-lit theaters by night. The freedom of a Court, presided over by an Emperor who still had the manners of a president anxious to please, set an easy example for light-hearted citizens. Damien, however, saw nothing to envy:

"Of course you are anxious to hear how things are going on in Paris. It is very seldom I go out in the town. Every Wednesday we go for a walk in a wood at some distance. About this wood I could say a great deal, as I know every avenue in it. About a thousand men are always at work there, in order to make it more and more pleasant. They make new roads, and dig small water-courses, so that the water may run in every direction. But, unfortunately, whereas before one could be quiet and enjoy the pleasures of a walk, now we see nothing but gentlemen and ladies, riders and carriages at every turn, which are a great distraction and annoying. What walks there are in the town have no longer the attraction for me which they had at the outset; to my mind there is something very melancholy about them. So whenever there is any question of a choice as to our walks, I always leave the streets to those who are more curious than myself. In our community everything is going on splendidly. We are all as active as hares, and get on capitally with one another. The arrival of one of our missionary bishops has given us an opportunity of having Pontifical Mass in our chapel. It was on Easter Sunday, and was the first time I had seen this solemn ceremonial. Instead of two or three priests, twenty or twenty-five were at the altar. In the evening after Vespers, the chapel was full of soldiers. The good bishop delivered a short discourse, gave them his blessing, and then came Benediction. The soldiers sang and served at the altar—in fact, did everything. They themselves were delighted. I believe this zealous missioner will shortly return to his mission in Oceania, and may possibly take some of us with him. Would you not be happy if I were to be one? . . ."

His mind continued to dwell on the possibilities of his going to the Southern Seas. The Bishop had painted a vivid picture of life in Oceania: the natural beauty of those far-off places, the undeniable glamour of tropic seas and coral isles, the swaying palms and scented flowers. Then as the hearts of the novice missionaries glowed, he had told them of the great field for future labor; theirs was the chance to combat, and change into good, the evil influences of those white men who had first entered into the island gardens, desecrating the happiness of the natives with spoliation and disease, immorality and the savage appetites of greed.

The ambitions of service, so long in Damien's head, now had a definite objective. Long letters filled with enthusiasm went to the ever-sympathetic Pamphile, and the brothers made plans to see the South Seas together. Meanwhile the duties in Paris were attacked with unremitting labor. Long hours at the desk brought inevitable results. That summer the young cleric was squinting with difficulty at the markings of an oculist's chart. From that date onwards he looked at the world through thick silver-bound spectacles.

Autumn snow was drifting down when he returned to Louvain to confront the final hurdles of advanced theology and philosophy. Again the brothers shared a room and together haunted the lecture halls. The University of Louvain is a noble and ancient institution, founded in the seventh century for the purpose of teaching medicine, law, arts, and theology, with particular emphasis on the last. The fact of being a student at the great university, in the company of brilliant scholars and famous professors, seems to have filled Damien, ever conscious that he was but a plodder, with awe and humility. Once he said to his brother: "When I am at the lectures the sight of so many clever fellows makes me veritably ashamed."

This year of his schooldays probably contained less hardship for Damien because Tremeloo is but a short distance from Louvain. It was possible for the brothers to make short visits to their home—occasions that were family events. At such times Madame de Veuster prepared huge meals. Relatives and neighbors rode in, under the wide skies of Flanders, to congregate at the farmhouse festivities. On one of these visits the opportunity came for Damien's first missionary effort. His father, as has been seen, was a good man and led a fixed life, particularly routine as far as religious devotions were concerned. He did what he considered was his duty, attending Mass and other devotions at the prescribed times and frequenting the Sacraments on such popular occasions as Easter and Christmas. But his younger son thought Communion should be received at least once a month, and after several long discussions the parent, first amused, then convinced, acceded to the son's wishes.

A momentous event for the family came when Pamphile was to celebrate his first Mass. Ten relatives, including, of course, the father and mother, journeyed to Louvain for the solemn and happy occasion. Damien was serving, and Madame de Veuster wept unashamedly with honest emotion as she watched her sons step to the altar. Even the father's eyes were moist as the age-old words of ritual were intoned by these men he had watched from cradle days. "*Benedicamus Domino*" said Pamphile. And their simple hearts surely must have responded in unison when Damien made the liturgical reply, "*Deo gratias.*"

This same chapel contained a stained glass window on which was a likeness of St. Francis Xavier, the gallant missionary-explorer of the sixteenth century. To him, as Patron of the Propagation of the Faith, the brothers had addressed many a prayer, begging his intercession that they, too, might soon preach and work in lands beyond the seas. The pleas were not entirely unheeded, for that summer the news sped around the monastery that the Bishop of the Hawaiian Islands had made an urgent demand for more missionaries. Who would be the lucky ones? There was an eager scurry among the young clerics; and the two brothers prayed more fervently than ever. Then, one hot July day, the news was made known. Ten *ordained* members of the community had been selected. Pamphile was notified that he should be prepared to sail in early October.

The disappointed Damien was told that, as he was still in minor Orders, and not yet an ordained priest, he would have to await his ordination before he could even think of going abroad, and it seemed certain that this contingent to the South Seas would be the last for many a day to sail in that direction. In the refectory it was whispered that for the next decade the Order's missionaries were to be sent to South America. Gallantly Damien tried to mask his own sorrow with a show of gladness at his brother's good fortune, but his heart remained heavy. He had been sure, so sure, that his destiny lay among those distant isles. Cheerfully he went about the business of assisting Pamphile to prepare for the long journey. Both knew that the separation would probably be for life, but, with the stoicism characteristic of their family, little was said about it.

The days drew nearer to autumn and the packing commenced in earnest. In the scant boxes allowed to be taken on the ship, there were a great variety of objects to be stowed: rosaries and trinkets to win the confidence of pagan children, clothing for hot climates, medicines to ward off fevers. Pamphile, however, did not have to wait for tropic zones to become familiar with fever. An epidemic of typhus, with all the horrors and confusion of sudden plague, swept through Louvain, leaving hardly a residence uncontaminated. As priests and doctors rushed to their duties, the dreadful rumble of death-carts became part of the town's familiar noises. The administration of the Last Sacraments to the dying, among the most virulently infected surroundings, became a shockingly repetitious rite for the newly ordained Père Pamphile. Deathbed after deathbed was visited in rapid and dangerous succession, until he, too, inevitably succumbed. As the tides of his fever rose and fell, it was his younger brother who kept vigil over the sick-bed and nursed him back to safety; a safety, however, that involved a long and careful convalescence.

It became only too evident that Pamphile could not stand the rigors of a long sea voyage and that he would have to give up his place among the missionaries. But who was to fill it? There were long talks in the sick-room, and, again and again, the brothers conspired to further Damien's career. Violating the rule of the Order, and guarding against any possible refusal from his immediate superiors, Damien addressed to the Superior General in Paris a fervent plea to be allowed to take his brother's place.

Long days of waiting followed; unhappy days, troubled with the anxiety of the unknown reply and disturbed by the consciousness of his first deliberate transgression against the rules of the Order. Then, one morning, as the students sat at their breakfast, the Superior of the community entered the refectory. His manner was stern, and Damien, already distraught, grew more uncomfortable as he realized that the cold eyes had turned to him. The dignitary walked across the room to where Damien sat and the clatter of dishes lessened respectfully.

"It is rather foolish for you to want to go before you are a priest, but you have your wish. You are to go!"

Damien heard the frigid voice. He did not hear the disapproval. (The Superior's coldness was, though justified, only momentary. Later, he was to write of Damien: "His regularity from the beginning was such that no eye, however vigilant, could ever find a fault in him.") All that Damien had heard was that his prayers had been answered.

"*You are to go!*"

Damien's heart sang and he thanked God.

CHAPTER II

He heard unfamiliar sounds: the harsh rasp of block and tackle under strain, the rattle of heavy chains, the screech of gulls diving at galley swill. There were equally strange smells: ship smells, tar and fresh paint in confined spaces, the rancid complaint of disturbed bilges, the odor from the brine barrels of pork and beef lashed in the alleyway outside the cabin door.

It was early afternoon, and Damien, squatting on an uncomfortably narrow bunk, was writing a letter to Tremeloo. Proudly he wrote in large letters the name of the port, Bremerhaven.

"We dined for the first time with our captain; he received us very kindly. We are treated first rate, and want for nothing. Five good Fathers from Paris take the greatest possible care of us. It seems to me that we have clothes enough for at least three years. We have very small cabins, in which there are two berths placed one above the other. Our life on board will be as if we are in a monastery; we shall keep the same rules as at Louvain. We shall have our first hours for prayer, study and recreation in the saloon which serves as a refectory and for all else we have to do. At noon on Saturday we expect to leave the harbour, trusting ourselves to Providence and to the direction of an experienced captain, who has made this voyage every year for the last seven or eight years. His name is Geerken. Although a Protestant, he is very kind to us and always dines with us. There is only one passenger besides ourselves . . . Do not trouble yourselves in the least about us. We are in

36

the hands of God, of an all-powerful God, who has taken us under his protection. All I ask you to do is to pray that we may have a good voyage, and that we may have courage to fulfill our tasks everywhere and at all times. That is our life! Good-bye, dearest parents. Henceforward we shall not have the happiness of seeing one another, but we shall always be united by that tender love which we bear to one another. In our prayers especially let us often remember one another, and unite ourselves to the Sacred Hearts of Jesus and Mary, in which I remain ever your affectionate son, *Father* Damien."

With a flourish he signed his name and title, particularly the latter, for he was still young enough to show a very human pride in the titular privileges of his vocation and at that time members of the Order were allowed to call themselves Père, even before actual ordination. He sealed the letter, then awkwardly climbed from the bunk. This last movement was performed with great care. There was not much room in the tiny cabin, which was to be his home for the next five months, to allow of any great freedom to his sturdy frame. Taking his broad, low-crowned hat, he went on deck which, to a landsman's eye, presented a scene of incoherent confusion and incredible disorder.

The broad beam and short length of the stout-hulled merchantman was alive with the activity inseparable from the last days in port of a sailing ship about to depart on a long voyage. Seamen, not always quite sober, swarmed up and down the tall masts under the ceaseless urgings of hoarse-throated officers. Endless chains of longshoremen, carrying stores, poured over the thick, high bulwarks. Rising above the general din, was the ceaseless hammering of the shipwrights and the squeak and lament of the live provisions—pigs and one cow cooped abaft the forecastle head. Damien gazed, fascinated, at the web of ropes and spars that almost obscured the sky, marveling at the great knowledge that it must take to control such a machine of wood and hemp, fashioned by men and driven by winds.

"Stand by below!"

A seaman unceremoniously elbowed him out of the way as a coil of thick rope hurtled down from above.

"Good morning, Father."

The Captain, a broad-faced German, with a seaman's hearty manner and with the shoulders of an ox, good-humoredly piloted him to the safer zones of the poop deck.

"Bon jour, Père Damien."

A group of nuns fluttered by, bound for the same security. These were fellow passengers, en route to found a boarding school of the *Dames des Sacrés Coeurs* at Honolulu.

Between the after-rail and the ship's wheel he found his friends. All were high-spirited and apparently very gay. None of them had ever been on a ship before. The prospects of the voyage, both perilous and long, thrilled and excited them. Good-humored jokes passed back and forth as the terrors of sea-sickness were discussed. As the sound of clerical laughter was heard, the crews of passing ships pulled long faces and muttered gloomy prophecies; according to an age-old superstition of the sea, the laughter of a priest brings bad luck to a ship's company.

The wind came that was to drive them half-way, and further, around the world. It was a chilly November morning and a slight mist softened the view of the crowded harbor. Gaskets were loosened and canvas billowed to the bawling of outward-bound chanteys. The missionaries huddled at the rail to wave their last goodbyes, and an inbound Spanish barque dipped her colors in respectful salute at the sight of so many cassocks. The tug, her giant side-paddles threshing noisily, cast them loose and the ship was suddenly free of the land.

Damien thrilled as the planks beneath him lifted to the swell of the open sea. The ship seemed to take life as cloud after cloud of white canvas was unleashed from the yards, to be instantly sheeted down; her decks became ordered; hatches were battened and lines coiled neatly; and the motto that was engraven on the binnacle began to take on meaning: *A place for everything and everything in its place.* Outward bound! Magical words to even the most hardened seaman, certainly magical to those young missionaries. The sun broke through the haze and the ship became suddenly beautiful, her brass and varnish gleaming, as she gathered speed and slanted to the waves. The tug had been left far behind and a melancholy blast from her siren was Europe's last salute to the voyagers. The breeze freshened and showers of spray began to wet the forecastle head. Behind them, the ship's wake, broad under the stern, narrowed to a distant nothing. Gradually the land was lost under the sea-line. The passage had commenced.

Damien paced the deck, getting his sea legs under the advice of Captain Geerken (who seems to have taken a fancy to him from the beginning). Most of his companions, already sea-sick, had sought their berths. Damien, alone of the group, was to suffer very little from that malady. He stared ahead at the boundary line where the sea met the sky, a line which never seemed to get closer for the next five months. What destiny had the Divine Being arranged for him beyond that elusive frontier? He prayed that, whatever it was, he would not fail.

Sea life came easy to him, the disciplined routine being not unlike that of the monastery. Those were the days of long passages and nobody seemed to mind. "The more days, the more dollars" sang the seamen. The ship was apart from the world, a world in itself. Bells tolled and divided the rotating hours and each man followed his appointed task. Damien liked the peace of the night watches: the lookouts, mute and alert, standing forward against the stars; the immobile face of the helmsman in the ghostly light of the binnacle; the measured tramp of the mate.

These were the things he liked and to him it seemed an ideal state of affairs; long peaceful hours when men were awake, but silent, using their voices only for the necessities.

This voyage was to leave its mark on him. In after years as he gazed out upon the sea that was the wall of his self-made prison he was often to speak of ships and the men who sailed them. With them he felt a curious comradeship, and they in turn had a respect for him that was not alone due to his cloth. Climbing had no terrors for him. When there was work to be done aloft, he would be seen, soutane tucked high, clambering up the swaying rigging with the seamen. He was to know the exultation of fighting canvas on a spar tossed with the fury of a squall and he was to experience the exhilaration of resting on the royal yard, high above the deck, above the sails themselves, in the bright sunshine of the early morning. There he felt completely happy.

Besides their devotions and a well arranged routine of studies the young clerics had each been given certain other tasks to perform. Damien had been appointed sacristan for the voyage. In this capacity he had to prepare the vestments used at Mass, look after the sacred vessels, and erect and dismantle the portable altar each time Mass was celebrated. This, of course, was a daily event and sometimes a very difficult one if the weather was rough. At one time during the voyage the supply of Altar Breads became exhausted but Damien was not daunted. Always resourceful, he enlisted the aid of the steward; after several attempts, and the spoiling of much flour, he managed to concoct a usable batch of wafers. And, although not yet obliged to do so, he assumed the priestly obligation of daily reciting the Divine Office. To his devout mind, a breviary was a treasured possession; it had everything that served to inspire his faith: passages from the lives of Saints, prayers and psalms, stirring extracts from both the Old and the New Testaments.

The ship sailed on, escaping winter in warmer latitudes,

and Captain Geerken walked the deck and talked religion with his young friend. The spirit of the missionary burned strongly in Damien and he scented a convert. His zealous attempts along these lines both amused and interested the wily old Protestant who, however, remained evasive. Like many shipmasters, he carried an excellent library and was by way of being a scholar, and it was he who introduced Damien to a German translation of Macaulay's famous criticism on Von Ranke's *History of the Popes*. Some of the historian's epigrammatic reasoning was too complicated for the young Fleming and some statements he soundly disapproved, but there were other portions that delighted him. The book was borrowed and with great labor the paragraph which caught his fancy was translated, by the aid of a dictionary, into both French and Latin!

"The history of that Church joins together the two great ages of human civilisation. No other institution is left standing which carries the mind back to the times when the smoke of sacrifice rose from the Pantheon, and when camelopards and tigers bounded in the Flavian amphitheatre. The proudest royal houses are but of yesterday, when compared with the line of the Supreme Pontiffs. That line we trace back in an unbroken series, from the Pope who crowned Napoleon in the nineteenth century to the Pope who crowned Pepin in the eighth; and far beyond the time of Pepin the august dynasty extends, till it is lost in the twilight of fable. The republic of Venice came next in antiquity. But the republic of Venice was modern when compared with the Papacy; and the republic of Venice is gone, and the Papacy remains. The Papacy remains, not in decay, not a mere antique, but full of life and youthful vigor. The Catholic missionaries as zealous as those who landed in Kent with Augustine, and still confronting hostile kings with the same spirit with which she confronted Attila . . . She saw the commencement of the governments and of all the ecclesiastical establishments

41

that now exist in the world; and we feel no assurance that she is not destined to see the end of them all. She was great and respected before the Saxon had set foot on Britain, before the Frank had passed the Rhine, when Grecian eloquence still flourished at Antioch, when idols were still worshipped in the temple of Mecca. And she may still exist in undiminished vigor when some traveler from New Zealand shall, in the midst of a vast solitude, take his stand on a broken arch of London Bridge to sketch the ruins of St. Paul's."

Copies were put into a letter to be sent to Pamphile. (That correct priest duly received and returned them with a literary frown made by underlining and putting several question marks after the phrase—". . . the august dynasty extends, till it is lost in the twilight of fable.")

Tropic doldrums were reached and the ship drifted uncomfortably as sails slatted and pitch boiled in the deck seams. Gravely Captain Geerken pasted a horsehair across the lens of his telescope and exhibited a visible Equator to the priests. A pagan god, King Neptune, in the form of the ship's boatswain, came aboard and with his noisy court exacted age-old tribute from landlubbers. There were the usual boisterous duckings and play, and the young missionaries submitted good-naturedly to a tax of two bottles of wine. Below in the sweltering heat of tiny cabins the nuns spent patient hours uncomplainingly. There was too much disporting of hairy limbs and flamboyant tattooings for them to be on deck.

The wind came again and the ship plowed still farther south and as the Horn came closer the waves danced higher and a chill came back into the air. The wind grew stronger and the careful Captain furled his royals and top-gallant sails. The narrowing latitudes changed and sudden winter, harsh and cold, descended upon them. Hatches were closed and life-lines rigged and the passengers were forbidden the deck. The seas no longer danced; they were now mountains that towered ominously. Over their peaks and into their valleys the ship lurched and two helmsmen at the wheel were lashed there for safety. The skies became dark with threatening shadows and, as Captain Geerken, bundled in oilskins, pointed an unsuccessful sextant at pale openings in the storm torn clouds, the wind became a gale. He worried for his ship as they ran blindly off the Straits. Cape Horn is notorious among seamen but this rounding, he afterwards declared, seemed to be the worst in his experience. The ship labored terribly as avalanches of seas rushed on board with all the force of broken dams. Seas on decks, seas on all sides, fought angrily to sink her. Gear was carried away and men were bruised and hurt. The weather showed no signs of abating and the seamen began to despair.

Down in the battered, wet saloon the missionaries had appealed for Divine assistance. A novena had been started at the commencement of the bad weather and exactly on the ninth day (February 2, 1864), as the Protestant sailors stared in astonishment, the gale began to lessen and the Captain pronounced that the danger was over.

They were now in the Pacific and as the course was changed to a northerly direction, the ship had recovered enough of her normal routine for Damien to resume a letter to Pamphile in which he made the time-honored joke about the Pacific not being so pacific. The sun soon became warmer, hatches were opened, clothes were dried, and singing could be heard in the evening watches again. The nights were very pleasant and the stars seemed very close. Once again the Equator was neared and crossed, and the Sisters kept discreet eyes to seaward as bronzed torsos were unbared.

The ship sailed on and the sun stayed kind. The missionaries read their breviaries, walked the decks, and got used to porpoises and flying fish flashing from the sea. They had been in the ship five months now and life on board was becoming irksome. Then, one day, to the accompaniment of loud hurrahs, a mountain grew from the horizon and, as the ship sailed closer, it broadened, becoming green and incredibly beautiful.

To sea-tired eyes it seemed like an enchanted island. It was the end of the journey—March 18, 1864.

CHAPTER III

The Hawaiian Islands, twelve in number, of which only eight are inhabited, lie two thousand miles west of the North American continent and about three and a half thousand from Japan. Volcanic in origin they were re-discovered by Europeans when Captain Cook landed there in 1778 to be received with great hospitality by the inhabitants, who thought he was a deity of some kind. This impression of divinity persisted; and even after they murdered him the following year, they placed his bones and other relics in their temples and treated them with great reverence. There is some credence placed in the claim that a Spaniard landed and settled on the island of Hawaii in 1555 and it is a fact that the Islands are correctly marked on seventeenth-century English charts. Cook named them after his patron, the Earl of Sandwich, and as such they remained on many charts until a comparatively recent date.

The natives are of the Malayo-Polynesian race and are believed to have settled in the Islands somewhere about the tenth century, coming from Samoa and, before that, from Tahiti and the Marquesas. However, little is actually known of their history, and those fragments are based upon legends passed from generation to generation. There is a strong link of language between them and the Marquesans and the Maoris of New Zealand; some attempts, without success, have been made to prove that this language is Aryan in origin.

At the time of Cook's arrival, the island group was divided into three separate kingdoms. Although a well-disposed people, and having some culture of their own (for

45

example they tilled the land and had a well-executed system of irrigation), they were still possessed of several barbaric customs. Cannibalism, although their defenders now deny it, was practiced in certain religious rites, and so was polyandry and polygamy. Descent was traced through the female line, but to offset this advantage innumerable taboos were foisted on the women. As late as 1810 females were forbidden, under penalty of death, to eat bananas, cocoanuts, turtles, pork or certain fish. Despite these dietary restrictions, the reports of the early mariners describe the women as being enormously fat, so great in bulk that for them, like Henry VIII in his later years, even walking was difficult. These descriptions, of course, applied only to the matrons, the young women being renowned for their charms.

In 1792 Captain Vancouver, considered by all to have been a great benefactor of the Islanders, helped the then King of Hawaii, an able and ambitious potentate, to build a ship of European design, the *Britannia*. Soon the monarch had a fleet of small vessels; within the decade, after subjugating the entire group, he was proclaimed Kamehameha I, King of the Islands—founder of an unfortunate dynasty. His death was the ending of the taboo system, and in 1820 his successor, clad in a simple costume that consisted of silk stockings and cocked hat, listened with an open mind to a band of missionaries from Boston. Up to that time, with the exception of Vancouver, the outside world had brought little to the Hawaiians except rum, firearms and notorious exhibitions of debauchery and vice. It was the vaunted arrogance of sea captains "that neither the laws of God nor man existed west of Cape Horn." With the arrival of the New England missionaries the country adopted European methods of administration and government with astonishing rapidity; and after several "incidents" the Powers recognized the Kingdom as such until the formation of a Provisional Government in 1893, followed by the farcical Republic a year later and the inevitable annexation by the United States in 1895.

Unfortunately, like the history of larger and older nations, the story of the Islands is not complete without its record of religious bigotry. Seven years after the Protestants landed, Catholic priests arrived; then in 1831 those latter were banished, through no fault of their own. With bravery and persistence they returned again in 1836 and the next two years were exceedingly hazardous for them, becoming critical, until the French frigate *Artemise* dropped anchor in the harbor. Naval officers of all nations, from Cook to Togo, were continually to have altercations with the Government until the annexation; and the Commander of this vessel, a swashbuckler called Captain Laplace, proved no exception. Flying an extra large ensign and dressing his ship as though it were a gala occasion, he trained his guns on the port town and threatened to level it to ruins unless His Majesty, King Kamehameha III, signed an agreement, insured by a cash indemnity, to cease molesting the Catholic missionaries and to guarantee them the same toleration as shown the Protestants.

This act of "gunpowder" diplomacy was successful and in a few years Catholicism was firmly established, becoming in time the seat of a Vicar Apostolic.

The dignitary occupying that position at the time of Damien's arrival was Msgr. Maigret. When he heard of the arrival of the missionary ship he hurried down to the waterfront. Captain Geerken, not caring to make port in the evening darkness, had remained outside the harbor all night while his passengers, too excited to sleep, sniffed the shore breeze laden with the sweet fragrance of tropical flowers, and, with imaginations stirring, watched the lights of the town till the advent of the new morning, a morning that still further excited them with splendors revealed by a closer view.

Sails had been furled and the ship rolled gently to the swell. On lofty perches sailors pulled at gaskets and regaled each other with impossible stories of Kanaka hospitality, while below them the missionaries clustered by the rail to watch the arrival of the official launch, bearing the port authorities. Other craft came, too, scores of canoes carrying crews of golden-skinned islanders, although these were not the fierce savages that somehow Damien had half expected; they seemed gentle and extremely friendly, tossing flower wreaths and shouting greetings to the deck.

The arrival of a ship has always been an event to Hawaiians and even in these modern times when steamships are a busy traffic in Honolulu waters, the arrival of a passenger liner is certain to be treated with ceremony. Therefore, it can well be imagined how joyfully that sailing ship from Bremerhaven was received. Gifts were brought aboard and literally showered upon the confused missionaries: huge bunches of bananas, golden pineapples and other exotic fruits and flowers that were as yet nameless to them.

Once again the decks lost the appearance of orderliness as mooring lines were uncoiled and preparation for the port was made. A tug took the ship in tow and a shore pilot directed the helmsman. Despite these assurances, however, the cautious Captain had men in the chains, starboard and larboard, hurling the deep-sea lead; and their voices, chanting in sea jargon the depth of the water, rose high over the babble and noise of the natives who were now swarming aboard by the hundreds. Small boys, like shoals of golden dolphins, swam out from the reef as the vessel entered the channel, their shrill cries increasing the general clamor.

The Captain, striding from side to side of the poop deck, noticed Damien leaning over the rail and gazing with entranced eyes at the antics of the swimmers. Pausing for a moment, the mariner informed him that the total native population of the Island was estimated at well under fifty thousand, whereas at the time of Captain Cook's arrival, they had been numbered at four hundred thousand! The appalling decrease in less than nine decades, hardly much longer than man's allotted span of years, had been caused by the triple scourges of consumption, syphilis and leprosy, diseases unknown before the arrival of the white man. Damien never forgot the Captain's grim statement; it saddened him with a sense of both shame and guilt at being one of the race that had committed this great wrong—a crime for which he eventually was to give in personal atonement the utmost a human can give.

By eight o'clock the ship was secured. The newcomers kissed the ring of the Vicar Apostolic and took leave of Geerken and the crew. Then they were escorted ashore where there was a great deal of merriment occasioned by what seemed, to feet and balance used to decks, the swaying motion of solid land. Even the gait of the nuns, sedate as they tried to make it, was marked with a slight roll.

They were taken to the Cathedral through streets that were unlike any they had seen before, narrow and crooked, branching in every direction and shaded with overhanging trees. After the desert of the sea their eyes drank in hungrily the profusion, the richness of the exotic foliage. Green of myriad shades, from pale to dark, is everywhere in Honolulu; green upon green punctuated with the scarlet of the hibiscus, the yellow of the Golden Shower, and the crimson crown of the *ponciana regia*. Not one of these plants was known to Damien. The people whom he saw on the streets were equally strange and picturesque; barefooted, scantily trousered native urchins, the mothers in the Mother Hubbard gowns introduced by the New England missionaries, the Mongol faces of Chinese immigrants still pig-tailed and skirted, the startling kimonos of Japanese women, sunblackened fishermen carrying the morning's haul in glittering iridescent heaps on the end of bamboo poles, red-faced English bluejackets and lantern-jawed Yankee merchants in starched white duck. . . .

Like a kaleidoscope of fresh wonders, the scene shifted continually before their wondering eyes until they arrived at the Cathedral. Here, the missionaries in the peace of the dim interior found a sudden transition from unreality to reality. In this alien land where everything was different they gratefully experienced a sense of home-coming upon entering the consecrated territory, for it is a happy fact that a Catholic church, whether it is a vast Cathedral, rich with centuries of history and tradition, or merely a tiny chapel, newly erected and poor, is always the same.

"In nomine Patris et Filii et Spiritus Sancti."
In gratitude for the safe voyage a Mass was said.
"Judica me, Deus . . ."
A priest intoned the familiar words, words that have come down through the centuries in the noble language that serves as a bond between Catholics,* be they Esquimo or Patagonian.
". . . ut meum ac vestrum sacrificium acceptabile fiat apud Dominum Deum . . ."
Damien was soon to say those same words before that same altar; for it did not take the Vicar Apostolic very long to realize that Damien was ready for the priesthood. Two months after his arrival episcopal hands were ceremonially imposed upon the young man and he received, in company with two others, the bestowal of that spiritual power which marked his final separation from the laity. To Catholic belief the priestly honors are divinely given and Damien was now no longer as other men; he was a priest, an inheritor of apostolic traditions and powers; he could offer the Eucharistic sacrifice and administer the sacraments; he was to preach, and, under the jurisdiction of his bishop, his was now the grave responsibility of hearing and forgiving the sins of men. He had received that dignity which, as St.

* Although Latin is generally supposed to be the sole liturgical language of the Church there are certain Uniate dioceses in southern Italy and the Eastern Church where other languages are permitted.

Gregory of Nyssa wrote in the fourth century, ". . . renders sublime and honorable him, who, by the Newness of Ordination, has been singled out from the multitude; he who was yesterday one of the people suddenly becomes a commander, a presiding officer, a teacher of righteousness, and the dispenser of hidden mysteries."

With full consciousness of the honor and obligation of his new office, Damien celebrated his first Mass the day * following his ordination. Such an occasion must be an event in the life of any new priest and it is not difficult to imagine the happiness that must have been Damien's as he approached the altar that day.

He is presiding at a rite that commenced with the Last Supper and was foretold by Malachias, the last of the Prophets. The Cathedral is full. All eyes are upon him, eyes that belong to men and women, who not so long ago practiced pagan rites before stone images, now watch this young man of an alien race who is bound to them by a common faith.

"In nomine Patris et Filii et Spiritus Sancti."

Slowly he makes the sign of the cross and utters the phrase he has ever dreamed of saying.

"Introibo ad altare Dei."

"I will go unto the Altar of God." With pride and sincerity he makes the liturgical declaration. The solemn ritual continues; he prepares the Sacrifice that is one with the Sacrifice of the Cross, and a hundred dark-skinned communicants press forward to receive the consecrated Host from his hands.

With pardonable pride he wrote to Pamphile:

"Recall the feelings you yourself experienced, the day you had the happiness to stand at the altar for the first time. Mine were the same with this difference, that you were surrounded by friends and brothers in religion; while I was surrounded by children, recent converts, who had

* Whit Sunday, 1864.

come from all parts to see their new spiritual fathers . . . strong were the emotions I experienced in giving for the first time the Bread of Life to a hundred persons, many of whom had, perhaps, been on their knees before their ancient gods . . ."

He had not to wait long before receiving a parish. Soon after his first Mass, Msgr. Maigret informed him that the field of his labors was to be the district of Puno on Hawaii, which is the largest and most easterly inhabited island of the group bearing its name. Within a few days he had embarked on a small inter-island steamer. Once again he walked a deck and felt the lift of the open sea beneath him; once again a ship, even though the voyage was short, was a prelude to the Unknown. It was his first steamer, and, not entirely without justification, he was suspicious of clattering engines and the mysteries of the stokehold.

There were other clergy aboard to keep him company; Father Clement who was about Damien's age and who had been ordained at the same time; and the Bishop himself who was conducting the pastors to their new posts. Msgr. Maigret, like his predecessor, Alexis Bachelot, was one of those missionary pioneers whose lives add to the history of the Church and whose courage is only equaled by their sound judgment. He was a leader who led, and every corner of the far-flung and difficult Vicariate was known to him. The routine of his life was a saga of adventure; a life spent making the rounds of his territory on the decks of tiny schooners or careening canoes manned with crews of two; a life risked innumerable times when making impossible landings on dangerous surf-beaten beaches. Throughout the Islands his purple sash was a familiar sight and the episcopal ring was saluted, not only by Catholics, but by Protestant sea captains and by pagan chiefs; for, although he laid no claim to any particular dignity, the actions of his everyday existence brought him deference and respect from all. Between such a man and

Damien it was only natural that a mutual liking sprang into being; they had the same capacity for hard work; the same practice of actions without words. Maigret kept an eye on the young man during their short voyage; he watched him during the years of his first pastorate. The result of that long observation was the friendship and understanding between superior and subordinate that was to work so well during the years at Molokai.

Appropriately enough, Damien was to glimpse that Island, the shore with which his somber destiny was to be so strongly linked, from the deck of the steamer as he wondered about the future. But he gazed at the vast precipices and broken peaks with little attention, being more concerned with the tumultuous life that surrounded him. One does not have to seek the diversion of distant scenery aboard an inter-island steamer. There is an abundance of the picturesque to be found in the crowded confines of the small craft which resembles a floating village—the deck a market place packed with a noisy throng and littered with merchandise of all varieties bought in Honolulu. There is gaiety, guitars twang and the young people dance, roaring with laughter when the ship lurches. Men argue, children romp, and the old women gossip; and everybody, regardless of age or sex, is garlanded like a bride with wreaths of strong-scented flowers. Sleeping mats are placed by the scuppers; in long serried rows the less happy, those unfortunates to whom the roll of the ship is disagreeable, lie apathetically, heads propped on their baggage which usually consists of large bundles bound with flamboyantly colored shawls.

The eager eyes of the young priests drank in the strange sights that surrounded them while the Bishop, used to such things, told them anecdotes of his earlier days. Soon Maui, lovely and green, loomed up and the anchor was dropped off a coral white beach that fringed an island which seemed to be the South Sea Island of song and fiction. A tiny village nestled languidly in the dark shade amidst the rich vegetation, and what the novice missionaries saw of the place convinced them that life must be very easy for the pleasant inhabitants who had swum and paddled their canoes to meet them. The soil of their lovely island was, and is, extremely fertile, there was fruit for all, and the transparent waters of the surrounding sea gave startling evidence of innumerable varieties of obliging fish. In this near-Paradise, the natives had taken kindly to Catholicism and a new church had just been built. The three resident priests rowed to greet the voyagers and to tell them a feast awaited ashore.

The natives had prepared an elaborate repast for their Bishop and it was here that Damien was to taste his first native food: roast pig, cooked on hot stones; poi, the national food, in special calabashes; fresh, green cocoanuts, huge shrimps and succulent fish, baked whole in pandamus leaves. Long speeches were made, for the Hawaiian, no less than his white brothers, is enamored of oratory at banquets, and there was the ceremonial swirl of grass skirts as the villagers executed the decorous dance of welcome. Pipes were produced and, as the tobacco haze rose, the priests, of varying ages, gathered around the Bishop and, with the peace that descends upon men at such times, talked of their homelands which none ever expected to visit again. Unaccompanied, Damien slipped away to stroll among the shadows of the village. Narrow winding lanes were made darkly mysterious by the gloom of overhanging mango and banana trees. Little houses fringed the thick tropical growth, and from them curious eyes peered out upon the alien, following his every movement. Small children dodged at safe distance, following as he found the grim ruins that were once part of a fortified house belonging to the second Kamehameha.

In the morning he said Mass at the new church. Hardly had he removed the vestments when the steamer's whistle blew a peremptory recall. He had liked the peace of this village for somehow it reminded him of Tremeloo; then too he would have liked to have more time with the resident pastors for they could give him advice that he knew he sorely needed for his own district.

The villagers escorted the priests back to the ship and hung *leis* of red and white blossoms around their necks as farewell songs were chanted. Damien, inclined to chafe under the load of blossoms, was about to remove the wreaths that made his cassock seem so gay, but the tolerant Bishop, knowing his Islands, bade the young priest to let them remain.

Soon they were at sea again, but not for long. From the crowded lower deck came a shout, then pandemonium, as the passengers came surging to the upper decks, shouting with terror. Fire had broken out in the lower hold and wisps of smoke were already escaping from the hatches. Conrad, in *Lord Jim*, has described fitly the panic that can sweep through a vessel on fire. At such a time, the hysteria of a fear-crazed mob is more dangerous than the actual flames. Fortunately, unlike the Conradian characters, the Captain and officers of this ship displayed a cool courage, heading off the onslaught of passengers who rushed the boats, while the Bishop and two priests with remarkable calm, walked in among the mob, convincing them by example and soothing words that there was no actual danger and that the fire was under control. Confidence was restored, and the conflagration, eventually controlled, was fought sanely. The Captain was profuse in his gratitude to the priests and declared to them there was no doubt in his mind that without their courageous action matters would have gone an entirely different course.

The affair was mentioned in Honolulu and the steamer company was later to thank the Bishop publicly. All that Damien, with his flair for understatement, ever said about the incident was:

". . . scarce had we left the harbour when the ship caught fire. There was just time to extinguish it before the wood was burnt through, so the water did not get in. We turned back immediately, and once more found ourselves safe and sound at the house of our Fathers of Maui, where we had to wait till another vessel arrived. I, myself, was not sorry . . . to stay with them a few days and profit from their long experience."

The brief period spent with the good Fathers of Maui was the only practical experience that Damien was to have before being deposited in his own pastorate, the district of Puno, among the volcanoes of Hawaii. He found he was to be the only white man living at this part of the island, but he was not dismayed:

"I am sorry I am neither a poet nor a writer, to send you a good description of my new country. . . . The climate is delightful, so that strangers easily become accustomed to it, and generally enjoy better health here than in their own country. The archipelago is made up of eight islands, four of which are large and four small. Hawaii, the one on which I am stationed, is larger than all the others together. It is as large as Belgium, if not larger. In the center are three volcanoes, two of which appear to be extinct. The third is still active, and it is in the neighborhood of this that Providence has destined me to be placed. From one end of my district to another you have to walk on lava. . . . I think I shall require fully three days to get from one end to the other. In every direction there are little villages scattered about, and for seven or eight years there has been no resident priest. Before leaving, the Bishop told me that I must remember the mission was quite in its infancy. Indeed, I found no church in which to say Mass, but two are now in course of construction. . . ."

With this last simple phrase he covers the long months of what must have been heroic labor endured beneath the blazing sun, for he was builder, carpenter and even architect of those churches. No money did he have to purchase

56

materials, but was there not good wood growing on every side? He hewed and he carried and his muscles hardened; the sound of his axe echoed through the trees, and natives, convinced and impressed by this example, came to help. It is the nature of men, no matter of what race, to admire physical prowess; and tales were soon passed through the villages of this man's strength. It was said he could out-carry and out-lift any other man on the island; wisely he made no attempt to quell the rumor—with the result that many a gallant whose pride had been ruffled by the challenge came to compete with him. Plank-carrying contests were arranged, and, as the games went on, the chapels grew.

Meanwhile, he celebrated Mass on mountain side or in native huts, wherever a few of the faithful could be induced to gather, and his sturdy cassock-swathed figure became a familiar sight as he tramped through his little dominion. His sole luggage, strapped to his back, was a few necessities of apparel and a knapsack containing an altar stone and the various Mass furnishings. No place seemed too inaccessible or difficult for him to visit. He hacked his way through jungle thickness and his path took him by cratered regions where active volcanoes seethed threateningly. He inhaled the sulphur fumes and surveyed the lakes of fire with calm eyes, remembering (in a letter to Pamphile) that the Maui Fathers had said, "There is nothing like it in the world to give one an idea of Hell." For one used to the serenity of Flanders fields he seemed singularly undisturbed by the proximity of this earthly Hades, but he was less calm when confronted with certain other phenomena, not unconnected with the lower regions, that flourished in this territory. The easy-going standards of Polynesian morality seemed very loose to the young priest; the casual transference of wives between the men and the general promiscuity of the sexes was a practice that he did his best to erase. His efforts in this direction were tolerated and sometimes accepted, for on the whole the people, even those he referred to as "savages" and "heretics," liked this earnest white man who so patently labored only for their good.

A meager stock of simple medicines, given to him by the wise Bishop, was kept at his house for anybody's use. When there was sickness or death, no trouble was too great for him to undertake. In the native language (in which he was now fairly fluent) his name had been rendered Kamiano and to his brother he rejoices that as such he was welcome in all the villages. "I, for my part, like them immensely . . . apart from those two evils, inconstancy and incontinency, you could not wish for better people, so gentle, pleasant-mannered, exceedingly tender-hearted are they." The words of the Superior General, bidding the missionaries to look for the good in life, seem to have taken seed, for in seminary days he surely would have scented only the sins of these children of the sun, but now . . .

"They do not seek to amass riches, neither is there luxury in their diet or dress. They are exceedingly hospitable and are ready to deprive themselves even of necessaries in order to supply your every want, should you have to ask a night's shelter from them. Even heretics will treat a priest well if he comes to their house. . . ."

Such goodwill, combined with his obvious sincerity and patient labor, could not fail to have the desired results. There was a new interest in the Christian religion. He began to make converts by the score, but reception into the Church was not given lightly. He realized the dangers and trouble that could be spread by renegades and the careless, and before administering baptism he had to be quite convinced that the aspirant was sincere and had a full understanding of the responsibilities and privileges of Christian life. This rule he was always to follow. It was relaxed only in those cases when the applicant was grievously ill and unlikely to live.

As his congregation grew a horse was acquired. On this nag he galloped bare-headed, for he was quite used to the sun now, many miles each morning to say Mass in different places. The chapels were completed; and remembering perhaps the peaceful music of a distant countryside, he sends home instructions to buy "two small bells for my two new churches." Other chapels sprang up, in most cases merely leaf shelters supported by saplings; the parish was becoming organized but the missionary spirit of the pastor was still not satisfied. Work. Work. It is, even in those early days, the history of his existence. He was one of those men who are never happy unless their hands are occupied and his labors were never confined to spiritual matters alone. Continually he was occupied with axe, spade or hammer. The incredible record of incessant toil was never to cease until the interruption of death.

Without the winter discomfort of Northern climes the Christmas season came. The Fathers of the Island gathered together for a rare meal, and French and Flemish poured in eager sentences as the outside world was discussed. The new King in Honolulu had been inaugurated; a bureau of immigration and the importation of foreign labor was being encouraged to increase the production of sugar and rice. A war of brother against brother still wracked the great republic to the east of them, and letters from home told of how the Prussians were defeating the Danes. Damien, listening respectfully to his elders, became concerned at the wan appearance of Father Clement who had come to Hawaii with him; his fellow priest had had the fever and seemed weak and distressed by the climate.

Damien was twenty-five now and his parishioners brought gifts of fruit and fish as they came to help him celebrate his natal Mass. For many reasons they were rather proud of their hard-working pastor with his superb physique and unusual strength. They regarded with respect and no little awe his celibate life, for, according to the inherited beliefs of their fathers, men who led such lives were men who were more than mere humans and possessed of supernatural powers. And celibate he remained. No one, except the Rev. Dr. Hyde, with his slanderous accusations (which are dealt with later), has ever disputed that fact. But was he ever tempted to break his vows? He was a man and it is to be supposed that he had the temptations of men. In that tropic garden there were warm, intoxicating evenings, scented with the fragrance of flowers and full of the soft music of distant chanting. The maidens of Hawaii have never been known to be reticent with their charm and undoubtedly many a sly glance of coquetry was turned on the lonely white resident of Puno. There probably were temptations, and perhaps they were the reason for the self-imposed sentence of continual manual labor, for, with untiring energy under the blazing sun, fresh problems continued. Never for him was there the relaxation of a task completed. By that time his eyes were fixed on further goals.

The failing health of Fr. Clement gave Damien the opportunity to volunteer to exchange parishes. The new territory, called Kohala, was far larger than his own, being one hundred and eighty square miles in extent and, according to rumors that reached him, much more difficult to administer. Eventually, after an exchange of several letters and a few visits, he prevailed upon the other to accept the easier living, then the formal consent of the Bishop was asked and duly received.

Within a month he was ensconced in new surroundings, but it took him longer than that to survey his position:

"The first round which I have made of my district has convinced me that, if I wish to administer it as it should be administered, it will entail a great deal of exertion. It has taken me fully six weeks to make the visitation of the whole district. . . ."

But thinking of his predecessor he chivalrously adds that the parish surrounding the main church is:

". . . well-organized . . . and the church is made of wood and built by our Brothers in the time of Father Eustace. It is very beautiful inside. My presbytery, too, although it is made outside of *pala* leaves, is nevertheless commodiously portioned out for rooms. It has a little workshop, two bedrooms, a dining room and small reception room. Why, it is almost luxurious! . . . Certainly it seems ample for one who but a few years before rejected a monastic cot as being over soft. Meanwhile a restless eye is turned further inland where a pioneer priest had ventured in earlier days to build chapels . . . of leaves. Unfortunately they are all in ruins now. Heresy and idolatry have made serious ravages. . . ."

Here was work, indeed. In the remote villages astonished eyes opened wide as a broad-shouldered white man bent low over improvised altars and the sonorous sound of liturgical Latin echoed to the tree tops.

"*In nomine Patris et Filii et Spiritus Sancti.*"

"In the name of the Father, and of the Son and of the Holy Ghost." The sacred phrase must have sung in his heart as he hacked through jungle tendrils, as he slashed through the mud of torrential tropic downpours, as he climbed precipitous mountains, as he struggled with his horse through swollen streams. "How, think you," (he asks Pamphile) "do we perform the long journeys? Well, we have horses and mules. I have just bought two—a very good horse for 100 francs and a mule for seventy-five. But sometimes I have to go by boat or foot."

He heard of a distant settlement containing a few Catholics but bounded by steep mountains and sea-hemmed precipices and considered almost impossible to reach at this time of year. Such stories only served to challenge his initiative. How should he get there? The elder men of the village were consulted but they shook their heads and counseled him to wait several months for the right season, warning of rain that was more than rain, and telling formidable stories of impassable gorges. But he, thinking of the isolated Christians who had been denied the sacraments so long, could not wait and made his decision to go by sea. A canoe, which was merely a hollowed log, was obtained and two of the more venturesome spirits of the village were persuaded to accompany him.

The sea had the calm flatness of dawn when they sailed but as the sun rose higher the water became ruffled until finally, in the late afternoon, the canoe capsized. By this time they were well out to sea and the situation looked, and was, grave. Sharks abounded in these waters, the seas were mounting higher and dusk was approaching.

Panic-stricken, the natives were about to stake all in a desperate attempt to swim ashore but the calmer judgment of the priest induced them to stay by the canoe. It was well they did so, for fins appeared soon in ominous, narrowing circles. It was impossible to right the craft in the turbulent chop of the sea, but it could be propelled slowly by dint of much pushing and pulling. This they took turns at; in addition, continually making a commotion by splashing and shouting to keep off the sharks. Land was eventually reached and, after prayers of thanksgiving, Damien took stock of the sodden belongings that remained in the canoe. Little had been lost because with true Flemish caution he had,

"before starting properly fastened everything to the boat. Only my breviary, which I liked very much, because it was so complete and at the same time very light to carry about, was soaked all through with sea-water, so that I can no longer use it in my travels. I had enough of it for the day, and deferred my intended visit till the following week, and then went by the mountains. . . ."

It took him four days. The first stages were made by

horse and after the going became too rough for the steed he proceeded on foot with the heavy knapsack strapped to his broad shoulders. The trail took him to the sea and he then waded through the surf and swam the distance to the rocks where foothold could be obtained again and where he found himself to be at the base of a high and steep mountain. This he scaled by climbing on hands and knees, grabbing at grass and roots which were rotten and dangerous to the grip. Meanwhile rain came but he clambered on, slipping and falling, but remaining determined. The summit was reached but it was razor-edged and a precipitous ravine yawned under his eyes. There was no sight of any village nor, indeed, anything to show that men had ever visited these regions, and before him a second mountain, as high as the one just climbed, obscured the horizon. Still not daunted he refreshed himself with a few moments rest and after a hurried meal of fruit, tackled the dangerous descent that first had to be covered before the second mountain could be approached. Not only was there the danger of falling but there was a peril of being forced by the rains to remain in the gorge which would mean slow death by exposure and starvation; but a far slower and more horrible end was reserved for Damien and finally he scaled the second mountain, only to find a desolate plateau and beyond that still another hill! His hands were broken and lacerated; three finger nails had been torn out, leaving bloody and sore wounds. His feet were equally wounded for his boots had long since disintegrated and his face, indeed, his entire body, bore deep scratches from vines and tendrils.

Nothing that breathed seemed to frequent these dismal regions, no birds, no animals, although once he thought he heard, as if from another world, weird, hooting cries from the crag tops. He marched on, through the pelting sleet, through tendrils that cut his raw flesh, through mud that was sometimes waist deep. Finally, the third summit was reached. There was nothing nearer the gray sky than he, and the whole world seemed beneath him. He continued on; down he went, the steepness in the night blackness being twice as difficult as the ascent. Over precipices, rock by rock, tree by tree, he worked his way. Down, always down, to fresh depths, to new miseries. It was too much, even for this human, to bear. The limit of endurance was reached and he collapsed with fatigue and loss of blood.

Had he but known, his destination was near. In the morning his still unconscious body was found by natives who carried him to a stream and in the clear water revived him and cleansed his wounds, with the happy result that a day later he was on his feet again. His body might ache but there was work to do. A dying child was baptized, the village was inspected and arrangements made for a Mass to be said the following morning. The inhabitants were eager for spiritual benefits and he was kept busy the first few days with instruction and baptisms. Soon he was fit enough to return to the more populous parts of his district but he was not satisfied to leave the remote region with a mere memory of his visit:

"I asked them to build a chapel. They promised to do it and have faithfully kept their word. They went up the mountains and cut down some very fine trees, and fashioned the branches into timber for the building, not of a sort of a hut, as most of our chapels are, but of a regular chapel built entirely of wood. Here I had everything ready; but who was to raise a suitable edifice with these materials? To employ a carpenter from other parts was beyond any possibility, so I made the plan as best I could and commenced the construction myself with two natives. When these people have some one to guide them, they are not without ability."

He regretted that there was no glass to put in the windows and that, as there was no bell, the faithful had to be summoned by a conch shell blown by staunch lungs, but it was with enormous pride and a sense of great satisfaction that he affixed a large cross, "six and a half feet high," to the gable.

The people were happy, too; this building standing in the center of their huddled village and dedicated to their God, was the most permanent edifice in the community and it belonged to them. Eagerly they promised that the altar would always be tended and the building kept clean. But who was to officiate at the services when the priest had gone? He solved this difficulty by selecting two men who had been to school in Honolulu and by training them in a reading knowledge of the Epistles and Gospels of the different Sundays. It was a sad day and momentous occasion when the priest took leave of his few friends. The entire village, men, women and children, marched with him for the commencement of the journey, singing farewell songs. And two young men stayed by his side until his house was reached.

Homecoming meant merely a resumption of the continuous routine of endless riding and tramping through steaming forests, along the rocky coast. Not a corner of his territory was ever left unvisited for long.

"I am visiting a part of my district twelve miles from this place. There are about a hundred resident Catholics. Where am I to say Mass for these poor people? One small hut of straw, the entrance of which is only four feet high; the roof is perhaps ten. The wind freely enters from all sides, so much so that the candles are sometimes on a sudden blown out during Mass. The altar is exceedingly simple: four posts and a board, covered with the altar cloths, that is all. The people come for confession from very early morning. As there is no confessional, I have to seat myself as best I can and then go on hearing confessions until nine o'clock, when I sound my trumpet, nothing more than a sea shell, to call everybody to divine service, which then commences. It is very often in these small channels that one does most good."

Life was never to be without heroic moments for him. One early morning while galloping along the surf line he observed an apparently disabled craft drifting off the shore. Shading his eyes from the hot sun, he could make out that it was not the usual canoe of a native fisherman, but a ship's lifeboat. An oar trailed listlessly from a rowlock and across the tiller bar an unmoving body was sprawled.

The priest lost no time. Plunging into the sea he swam, unmindful of the sharks, to the boat. There a grim sight awaited him. Eight seamen, emaciated, sun-blackened, and in the last stages of exhaustion, lolled helplessly across the thwarts. He managed to beach the boat and drag the seamen to the shore, where, in the cool shade of low overhanging shrubbery, he stripped leaves and made couches. He brought fresh green cocoanuts and trickled the cool liquid down parched throats until the men revived to tell a story of fire at sea and eight days of horror in the open boat. There were four Englishmen, three Americans and a Dutchman, and they were Protestants; but they were also his welcome guests until a coasting vessel took them on to Honolulu. He enjoyed their company and the few pleasant evenings he spent, sharing his tobacco and talking to them in halting English (which he gradually was learning) of ships and life at sea.

CHAPTER IV

Vicissitudes occasioned by nature were not the only obstacles that made the way of the priest difficult. There were others, less obvious, but more powerful, and certainly harder to overcome. Rites of paganism still were practiced on the island, and many of Damien's community were still under the necromantic influence of native witch-doctors who were careful to keep their identity a secret. In ancient times those sorcerers, called *kahunas*, had been a highly revered and feared class—next in rank, and certainly not subservient in authority, to the kings. Indeed, they had grown so strong in power that just fifty years before Damien's arrival the Islands had been taboo-ridden to a degree that would have seemed ludicrous if the results had been less tragic. A *kahuna* had the power of life and death; as he was supposed to be in constant communication with his favorite divinity, he could issue a taboo at the slightest provocation. The only possible escape for the unfortunate transgressor of a priestly ban was to flee to a city of refuge; for, like the ancient Jews, the Hawaiians had these walled towns, bounded by temples, and all men, no matter what were their crimes, could find safety within the prescribed limits.

These island people seem to have had many other customs in common with the Israelites. Circumcision was practiced and their legends of the Creation are strangely similar to the Old Testament, although instead of one Deity a divine trinity existed at the beginning: Kane, the founder, Ku, the builder, and Lono, director of the elements. This Trinity created the earth and the Heavens, the sun, moon and stars, and from the earth clay a man was fashioned in the likeness of Kane. This and other similar stories were brought to the islands in the eleventh century by the high priest Paao, and passed from generation to generation by the successive *kahunas*.

Unfortunately, until the arrival of the missionaries, they never had any method of writing, not even picture-writing like that of the Egyptians and Aztecs. Where and how did the Hawaiian priesthood become possessed of these tales so strangely akin to the Hebrew narrative of the Book of Genesis? There are many theories but none of them has ever been satisfactorily proved. As the centuries rolled by, the Biblical tradition although still existing did not serve to prevent the formation of lesser divinities. War gods sprang into being and finally each trade or profession acquired its tutelar deity, and with them came innumerable gnomes and fairies, nymphs, monsters and evil spirits. The credulous people were at the mercy of any fakir with sufficient imagination to create a tale of superstition until, with the death of Kamehameha I, the power of the *kahunas* was broken and gradually as a class they were to perish. Nevertheless, for several generations, an occasional one persisted in the remote districts, forming cults the adherents of which met, in secret, to practise sinister rites.

Rumors of such a sect existing in his parish came to the ears of Damien; there were whisperings in the confessional of spells and fears and of ritualistic dances that were exotic and obscene. At deathbeds he sometimes had seen unmistakable evidences of the sorcerer's trade in the form of unclean tokens and charms. Although he campaigned vigorously and tried to discover the identity of the members and the whereabouts of the meetings his efforts were met with futility. Even the most faithful and earnest of his parishioners, as though they dreaded some supernatural revenge, would become uncommunicative before his queries and to his dismay the evil influences seemed to be spreading, rather than decreasing. Faces that had been friendly were turned away from him when he passed. Greetings were not answered, and the congregations at the chapel began to decrease. At funerals when he was reading the service he was conscious of a furtive air among the mourners as though other powers were being appealed to.

One night as he sat outside his house enjoying the peace of the evening and idly peering up at the spangled canopy of the tropical night, he heard distant drums that throbbed with an unfamiliar note; not the usual festive beat, but a rapid, disquieting tattoo. The sharp silence that followed an abrupt cessation of the noise was punctuated with an inhuman scream, then silence again. Damien, startled to his feet, stared at the direction of the noise in a state of angry alarm. He had been long enough in the island to know better than to attempt a search that evening; the following day he made a thorough exploration of the neighborhood and was rewarded by finding, hidden in a thicket of tree ferns, a strange and rudely shaped image of stone. In the cool green twilight caused by the natural roof of the giant fronds that met overhead he carefully examined the idol. It had a roughly hewn face and was obese and squat, standing about four feet tall and at the base was a flat rock, evidently an altar which was mottled with dark stains, still damp and thick, of clotted blood. The repugnant evidences of recent and gory sacrifice gave the priest added strength. Pushing against the image he toppled it over, smashing the altar beneath. Then with the clasp knife he always carried he slashed two branches from a nearby tree and lashing them together with vine tendrils fashioned a crude cross which he triumphantly erected in the place where the idol had stood. To leave no doubt as to who was responsible for this handiwork he left his clerical hat on the ground and in plain view.

The following day was a Sunday and in the church he delivered a bitter harangue that was both a denunciation and challenge against the sect of idol worshipers. He did not have to wait long for an answer. The next morning a sorcerer's talisman in the form of a small, oddly shaped shell filled with evil smelling ashes and bound with dried sinews was found tied to his door. Well aware that the eyes of the entire village were watching his every action, he took the token and with a great show of contempt tied it to the tail of a large hog. All that day the swine snouted and grubbed for food in the usual noisy way of such an animal, quite unaware of the abracadabra at its rump but in the evening it died; the corpse, revealing a throat cut in a jagged wound, was left at Damien's door. He tried to make a joke of the affair, saying that although the beast's death was the work of a poor butcher he was nevertheless grateful for the gift of fresh pork, even though it be from an anonymous donor. But the villagers refused to share his lightheartedness, no native could be induced to venture near the carcass, and indeed the man who acted as his servant vanished when called to help skin it.

Late that night as the priest lay tossing in his bed, kept awake and troubled with the difficulties of this new problem which was gradually diminishing and threatening to destroy his influence, the distant beat of drums suddenly intruded on his thoughts. He listened intently and then became conscious of a fresh sound; a faint scratching at the window. A woman was there, a timid, frightened creature —he recognized her as one whom he had once befriended by giving medicine to her sick child. With haste that was frantic and made her speech almost too incoherent, she whispered a few words; then, as though terrified and alarmed at her own rashness, she fled back into the shadows before he could ask further questions. But she had said enough. Incantation rites, a conjuring of evil spirits against his life, were being held at that very moment in a burial cave not far away.

It did not take him long to don shoes and cassock. Seizing a thick sturdy stick, which he sometimes used on tramping expeditions, he opened his door, only to pause at the threshold where after a moment's thought he deposited the stick back in its accustomed place, reasoning that it would be just as well to be completely unarmed as to bring such a poor weapon into the gathering he expected to find. After an hour's journey he arrived at the entrance of the burial caves which were on rocky shelves that protruded from the side of a small hill. The long walk through the darkness of thickly clustered trees on such an errand must have tried even his indomitable courage but he kept steadily on.

Muffled drums were beating. From the cave mouth a glare, wavering and of a pale reddish hue, gave a fitful illumination to the surrounding rocks. As he emerged from the tree shadows to the hillside he could hear, over the now loud savage beat of the drums, a wailing scream as though an animal was being tortured. Apparently the ritualists felt certain of being undisturbed or perhaps they were too absorbed in their gruesome functions; whatever the cause, there was no guard or sentry to prevent the priest clambering to the cave entrance and from there in the shadow of a giant boulder witnessing a weird scene.

Four tall, smoky, flaming torches were implanted in the center of the cavern floor. Their flickering light revealed a half circle of about thirty men of varying ages crouched, shoulder to shoulder, staring with fixed eyes at the shadowy end of the cave, where a ghoul-like figure was bent low, huddled at some task that Damien, in smoke-laden air, at first could not discern. From this individual came a muttered incantation. Flanking the cavern walls and squatting among human bones were the shadowy outlines of the drummers who were pounding at the shark-skin covered gourds in a rapid, unceasing tempo. On heaps of moldering kapa cloth, bones, startlingly white in the gloom, lay scattered everywhere in a terrible confusion of separate feet, hands and skulls. The air was almost unbreathable and stank of death. The walls were wet with a moisture that in the changing light glittered like slime-covered coal.

The incantation rose higher and Damien, his eyes becoming more accustomed to the murk, recognized the speaker as being one Mauae who had a reputation throughout the region as a hermit and a soothsayer. Shrunken and black, toothless and incredibly old, he was an evil sight at any time and actually was not Hawaiian by birth or blood but a dubious mixture of negro and Portuguese, born in the West Indies where, at a tender age, he joined the crew of an American whaler, which he had promptly deserted on arriving at the Islands.

As Damien watched, this individual straightened up to reveal that the object over which he had been crouched was the limp form of a small dog. Its throat had been cut and Mauae, holding the head of the unfortunate animal in a rigid position, spouted the blood into a large open gourd. When it was filled he relinquished the corpse and devoted his entire attention to the gory vessel, staring into it and screaming a supplication, swaying backwards and forwards as though trying to work himself into a trance. The gibberish that he chanted was in a language unknown to Damien, but the priest rightfully concluded that both it and the demonological ceremony belonged, not to this island, but to the country of Mauae's negro forbears. He strained forward in an effort to distinguish the words but with a disturbing abruptness the conjuration ceased and the witch doctor held up his hand in a signal to the drummers who also stopped.

The sudden silence that followed, broken only by the sound of heavy breathing, seemed unnatural; it was a silence laden with the weight of expectancy. Another signal was given and three of the torches were extinguished, leaving only one wavering smoke-crested flame whose shifting shadows made uneasy movements among the watchers. But their eyes remained fixed, in a rigid gaze, fascinated by fear, upon the dim figure by the gourd who now reached back into the shadows beyond the corpse of the butchered dog and drew out another object; a crudely fashioned puppet whose wooden face had been smeared white and which

72

wore a black cloth cassock-like gown. A tiny wooden cross was hung about the neck and a string of rosary beads that Damien had missed from his house some months before was fastened around the waist. There was no doubt but that the doll was supposed to be an effigy of the priest and the witch doctor gloated over it as he twisted back to the blood receptacle.

Damien did not hesitate any longer. Without uttering a word he plunged through the crowd which, stunned by his dramatic entrance, remained still for a moment of startled inactivity, then with a sudden uproar rushed at him but he, in his rage, made perhaps what was a very wise move. Seizing the puppet from Mauae he sent that individual reeling back with a violent blow that made him stumble over the gourd so that it upset, the contents spreading in a dark stain. The crowd stopped before the spilt blood. The din died quickly as they watched Damien with angry scorn rip the doll to pieces. Expressions changed from rage to fear, then to perplexity. It was obvious they had expected an awful catastrophe to strike the white man as he mutilated his own image. Nothing more terrible happened than a whining flow of curses from the cowering Mauae who, slinking in the background, was, despite his imprecations, plainly in fear of the priest.

Damien looked at the dark faces that surrounded him, shrewdly reading their thoughts. These men were the sons of men who before under the urgings of their *kahunas* had practiced the bloodiest of human sacrifices; there still were old men in the villages who boasted of having seen Cook's flesh burned on the altars; and if they had any faith in the wretched celebrant of the recent unsavory rite as a *kahuna* they would undoubtedly serve the same fate to him. Mauae must be thoroughly discredited. With a sudden, contemptuous gesture that made them step back in alarm the priest scattered the torn remnants of the doll over the floor. "Are you children that you are afraid of a doll and the blood of a dog?" he asked derisively. Then grinding his heel into the face of the puppet he illustrated undeniably that no harm could come to him no matter how much he insulted the Evil Spirits. Sullen faces became doubtful and sheepish, and nobody attempted to detain him when, after telling them that the air of this foul place was bad for honest men and that they should go home to their wives and children, he strode out of the cavern to walk the miles back to his own house, comfortable with victory.

After this incident there was little opposition to him. Soon the entire parish, like his first district, was active with unopposed Catholic organization. More chapels were erected, and to officiate at them he trained an entire class of lay preachers. Schools were needed. He appealed to the Government in Honolulu. At that time, because of the influence of New England missionaries, the authorities favored Protestant education, but reports had already reached them of this remarkable young man. They acceded to his request, sending four Catholic teachers with instruction that they should act under the advice and guidance of the priest. He wrote other appeals to Honolulu, and the surprised Bishop received a vast epistle that extolled the merits of seasoned timbers, not axe-hewn, but smoothed by skilled carpenters. Damien, like priests the world over, was dreaming of a larger and more permanent church, an edifice far beyond the primitive materials and financial capacity of his own Island. Lyrically did he write of the inspiration that the beauties of a stained-glass window would give his simple congregation, which with modest pride he pointed out was much too large for the present building.

Msgr. Maigret read the long pages and smiled contentedly, for reports had also reached him of Damien's progress; he was reminded that it was only thirty years since he, fleeing from Honolulu under sentence of banishment, had buried Father Bachelot at sea aboard the tiny schooner "Missionary Packet." The future had seemed very black then. Priests were in bad repute and their converts had been imprisoned and forced to work as scavengers. He had been jeered at and threatened and exiled, but he had returned; and the proof of his work was in such a letter as he was now reading. Thirty years and here was a young priest of a distant parish who wrote of crowded chapels and growing schools and the "absolute need" of a larger church! The Bishop smiled and showed the letter to the Mother Superior of the Sisters who had voyaged from Belgium with Damien. She remembered the young priest and after some talk it was agreed that a fund should be raised for the new church.

It was only two months later and all the materials had been purchased and were ready to be sent to Kohala. The wood had been cut and fitted for mounting by expert carpenters, a few sacred images, a small font, and a complete set of brilliantly colored Stations of the Cross waited in crates on the dock for the steamer. It was a great moment for the priest and his parishioners when that vessel hove in sight; the entire community had gathered at the coastal landing.

"You must know (he writes) that the place where this church was to be raised was on a hill, at a distance of nine miles from the sea. The coast is so rough that three pair of oxen had hard work to draw an empty wagon. Moreover, no road had been tracked here; we have to jump from boulder to boulder. The heat of the sun, too, is unbearable on this side of the hill. I thought, therefore, that the only means would be to have all my neophytes, men, women and children, come down in the evening. They slept on the coast in the open air, with their heads resting on stones; and, early next morning, everybody took up a load of timber, as much as he could carry, and then they all went up the hill. . . ."

It must have been a picturesque and stirring sight; the hazardous unloading of the precious cargo from the ship, through the surf to the rockbound beach; then the long winding column of burdened islanders, toiling up the hill, struggling across those giant boulders over which "no road had been tracked." The women and children, marching alongside the men, sang and helped and shouted happy encouragement. Damien, not content with directing the enterprise, carried a beam which no other man could even lift. At the village "the pieces were mounted as fast as they were brought up; this greatly encouraging everybody."

He was a great admirer of what he called "the imposing pomp of our solemnities," and the new edifice was carefully and elaborately decorated. Flemish thriftiness, combined with poverty and his intense practical sense, developed an astonishing ingenuity that produced a splendid and appropriate altar made from mother-of-pearl shell. Even the tapers were made in the parish, being molded from the produce of beehives that he had established in his garden. Pews he did not have to worry about, for the natives were unaccustomed to such articles of furniture and were content with mats.

Still his indefatigable energy was not appeased. In the same letter that he sent to Pamphile describing the building of this Church he adds, "Please God, I shall recommence the same sort of work next year in another part of my district, thirty miles from this last."

Such experience could not fail to mold more firmly both the moral and physical strength shown by him from the beginning. He was now nearing thirty, a frank-faced happy priest, sure of himself and his mission; this latter fact being, perhaps, the secret of the courage which inspired the Bishop, who was used to brave men, to refer to him as "the intrepid one." His health was superb; exercise, long journeys in the saddle, tramping over mountains and into valleys, and a frugal diet helped to keep it so. Hours were arranged with methodical regularity, he rose at daybreak and followed the day with an unvarying routine—except for such emergencies as sick calls—that ceased punctually at eight. He was popular and friendly with his parishioners but was careful to see that he gave no cause for a familiarity which might lessen the respect they had for him as a priest. To them, as to their forbears, men of God were a caste apart. Therefore, any moment of leisure that he might have, he spent alone. Tobacco was the only luxury he permitted himself. At first he tried self-discipline even in this harmless habit, confining his smoking to one pipeful a day; during the brief and treasured minutes before bedtime, the satisfying weed would be enjoyed to the utmost contentment as he either wrote or read letters from home. The latter were events that, on the lonely islands, were becoming far too rare and a gentle humorous reproof is penned to Pauline, now a nun in Holland.

"Three years now, and not a line from you. Where are you then, my dear sister? Are you off to Heaven already? Not so fast, if you please. A little more time is needed to win that crown. Take pity then on your poor brother, who, by dint of being so long forgotten, will soon become a regular savage among savages. Well, I certainly love my savages, who soon will be more civilized than Europeans. They are learning to read and write. . . ."

When a long overdue letter came from Tremeloo he told his parents: "for a long time I have been distressed and in suspense about you, not knowing what might have happened. I learn to my great joy that you are in good health. . . ."

It was a welcome break in his life when Monseigneur Maigret came to the island on a brief visit, bringing another missionary to take over half the district; it was obvious to the prelate that the mounting work was too great for one priest, even Damien, and that there were now enough Catholic interests to warrant two separate parishes. Even with the convenience and shortening of distances caused by the partitioning of the territory, Damien was still obliged to say three Masses in three different churches on

Sundays; each place being at least fifteen miles from the next.

In his new church he had improvised the semblance of an episcopal throne and there his Superior sat the morning after his arrival while the priest sang a High Mass in a deep voice that was well suited for the chanting of the sonorous phrases. But it was not the mere chanting of a splendid voice that impressed the Bishop; every note, every gesture that the service called for, bespoke an intense emotional power based on faith and this faith was plainly communicated to the large congregation that overflowed the church. At the moment of the Elevation there was, after the first movements of prostration, that silence of the devout that is somehow something more than a cessation of sound. No costly elaborations glittered at the island-constructed altar but it was handsome with tall brass candlesticks and snowy linens and delicate laces donated by the Sisters, and as Damien made his precise movements the Bishop looked back upon the sea of dark bowed heads and was happy.

The episcopal sojourn lasted for two months. Every corner of the parish was visited with the priest. There were celebrations, confirmations, and religious processions; thuribles swung and incense clouded the interior of remote grass-covered chapels. But it must not be supposed that the journey of inspection was a pompous march, marked with purple flaunting display or burdensome dignity. There were happy festivals of flowers and feasts, and despite the long distances the aged Bishop, still hardy with years of such living, would challenge the younger men to mule and horse races; in the early mornings surprised natives would be startled by the sudden thunder of hoofs as the ecclesiastical cavalcade galloped by. "And, [reports the awed, and perhaps wise, Damien] as his Lordship was one of the best riders of the company, he was generally victorious."

The visit ended and once again Damien was by himself.

His fourth Christmas approached on this island where except for warm, damp discomfort or incessant rain there was nothing to mark the changing of the seasons. Thoughts turned to a land across the seas. There would be real winter at Tremeloo, he reflected, not too harsh, but enough crispness in the air to make the blood tingle; the river Laak would be frozen to a hardness right for skating; in the farmhouse kitchen a bright fire would be blazing, giving cheerful glints to the burnished copper pots; his mother would be humming a Flemish song as she prepared the Christmas feast. He was grateful when the rare letters arrived and to one of them he replied:

"It is a great happiness to me whenever I have an opportunity of sending news of myself, of reminding you, my dear parents, that on an island in the midst of the great Pacific, you have a son who loves you and a priest who prays for you. . . ."

1870 came and there was much happening in the outside world to interest the exiled priest. The Vatican Council had defined the dogma of papal infallibility. The Suez Canal was a known success and poems were being written the world over, lauding the indomitable perseverance of the French engineer, de Lesseps. Other Frenchmen were seeking lustre too. Marshals flourished batons towards Berlin and German drums answered with tattoos of defiance. Damien was alarmed. "I hope Belgium at least will not be disturbed. . . . I grieve to hear of this war and pray that it will soon cease. . . ." But history, continuing its inexorable course, persisted to be written in blood, and at Sedan French cavalry charged with futile bravery. Once again a Bonaparte became a prisoner as William I received the sword of Napoleon III. Bestarred generals and ambitious dynasts, amidst the pageantry of war, might occupy the center of the world's stage, but less spectacular forces were also at work. Pasteur was peering into vats and prodding rabbits. In England a Miss Nightingale with the prestige of Scutari behind her, wrote letters of advice on nursing reform that echoed in the drawing-rooms of the great.

Sanitation and hospital administration became mildly fashionable topics and hobbies among the leaders of nations; and when the Duke of Edinburgh, visiting Honolulu, spoke of new institutions in his country, Kamehameha V was able to show him with great pride the new hospital named after the previous monarch's queen.

It was a fine building, comparable to any in Europe, but, unfortunately, it had no facilities to cope with the one disease that was the most dreaded in the Islands. Leprosy had been first observed in 1853. Ten years later it had spread to such an alarming extent that the authorities realized that some measures would have to be taken to segregate the afflicted and to fight the disease. Efforts in this direction were at first pitifully inadequate. A small receiving station was established near Honolulu, but such an uproar was raised by citizens, who dreaded the proximity of the lepers, that land was purchased on the island of Molokai in a peninsular region, bounded by the sea on three sides and sufficiently isolated to satisfy the most timid. In 1866 one hundred and forty lepers were sent there, not as patients, but as *colonists!*

Land was given to them, along with the essentials needed for farming. Then they were left to fend for themselves. They, those people with rotting limbs and horribly diseased bodies, were expected to till the soil and thus, according to the ingenious plan, be self-supporting and no longer a burden to the Government. Of course the absurd scheme was bound for failure and it was a failure that meant indescribable suffering and a fearsome death to most of the unfortunate victims. But, although impractical, it was cheap and for a time the zealous guardians of public money persisted with the fantastic colonization. More lepers, along with some paltry stores, were landed on Molokai, the result being a community that almost defies description. Those people, already doomed to death, had been exiled to die in surroundings and conditions they bitterly resented. Feeling that they were beyond the power of any earthly law, and having no knowledge or assurance of any other, they abandoned themselves to their fate with apathy alternating with orgies. Supplies were soon exhausted. The stronger stole from the weak. The agonies of the dying were made more acute with the cruelties of starvation and exposure. A species of native beer, foul to the taste, but strong to the senses, was easy to brew from the roots of a wild plant. Drunkenness became rife, rioting broke out. Soon there was no semblance of any order amongst scenes of incredible debauch and sexual license that always in macabre accompaniment had the unheeded cries of the dying.

A few of the inmates managed to escape and soon, around the islands, the truth about the dreadful place was made known. From the comfortable offices of the authorities in Honolulu commands were issued, but who was to enforce these commands? A superintendent was appointed but his efforts were met with open rebellion. Troops were sent but sentries who were not afraid of steel or powder ran flying before the lepers who used their open sores as weapons; two or three rushing a healthy man and enveloping him in ghastly embrace, rubbing their spittle and pus on his skin. The whole affair took on the aspects of a hideous, diabolically inspired nightmare. In the meantime leprosy continued to spread with alarming speed throughout the entire population of the territory. A new king came to the throne and his new Board of Health, shocked by a recent census, tried to improve conditions both in and outside the settlement.

The laws of segregation and quarantine were enforced rigorously. All suspected of the disease were ordered to report to the proper officials and prepare to go to the settlement. But the unsavory reputation of Molokai made this decree unpopular. The natives, always a family-loving people, could not understand why they should give up loved ones, whom they were quite willing to nurse and care for, to be delivered to what was rightly considered a hell on earth. But this time the authorities, determined to check the disease, were in earnest. Lepers were hunted by officials, usually white men, with great zeal. In consequence, whole families took to the hills and caves. Soon there were entire communities living in hiding. It must be said that, not without some justification, the sympathies of the bulk of the population were with them.

Damien's district was not exempt from the trouble. Just about this time he reported home that

"Leprosy is beginning to be very prevalent here. There are many men covered with it. It does not cause death at once, but it is rarely cured. The disease is very dangerous, because it is highly contagious. . . ."

Within a month after he penned these ominous words a doctor and four police officials arrived in his village and in a conspicuous place posted up the cold and tersely worded announcement:

ALL LEPERS ARE REQUIRED TO REPORT THEMSELVES
TO THE GOVERNMENT HEALTH AUTHORITIES WITHIN
FOURTEEN DAYS FROM THIS DATE FOR INSPECTION
AND FINAL BANISHMENT TO MOLOKAI.

The priest watched while the officials went about their grim and formidable task. For the next few weeks the village was a place of sadness. Whole families journeyed in from the outer districts to deliver a son or a husband, a wife or a daughter, to the white men in obedience to the law. They spread their mats in front of the church and there, in dejected clusters, waited for the final parting. Mournful sounds of continuous sobbing and wailing filled the air and there was an atmosphere of death, a funeral in which the dead themselves walked. With heavy heart

Damien performed his priestly duties, hearing confessions, giving absolution and administering the Sacraments. He had shown many of the deportees the value of these tangible comforts of religion; he had taught them the necessity of receiving the Sacraments; and now, through no fault of their own, they were being sent to a place where the likelihood of either physical or spiritual attention was exceedingly problematical.

As on the other islands, there were some who did not submit to their fate with peaceful resignation. In a few cases the police officials were forced to use harsh measures and the sad groups congregated outside of Damien's church were supplemented by manacled prisoners.

One man whose wife was said to have the disease took to a deserted ravine and there from behind an improvised fort defied the authorities. It was easy to sympathize with him; he was devoted to his wife and had cared for her in the best fashion that he knew, causing no trouble to anybody and dwelling apart from his neighbors in a hut on a lonely section of the coast. On hearing of the Government's proclamation he had taken to his hilly refuge and rather than have his wife sent to the notorious pesthole at Molokai he was prepared to offer a determined resistance. From an unknown source he had procured a rifle and ammunition. When the police attempted to advance on him they were met with warning shots and a threat that if they persisted the aim would be better the next time. A siege commenced; after a few days the officials made plans for a concerted rush, and it was certain that blood would be shed. Not wanting to see this happen, Damien interceded and begged that he be allowed to try to visit the determined native and persuade him that his opposition was useless. The officials after warning the priest that whatever he did was at his own risk granted the request. Immediately Damien commenced the ascent to the native's stronghold. He made no attempt to conceal himself, not even when there was a savage, angry report of a rifle and the terrifying ricocheting on the rocks about him. Three times the gun spat and then in the silence that succeeded Damien, still climbing, shouted, "It is I, your friend, Kamiano." There were no more shots, but when he reached the level of the stony rampart he was confronted with mistrustful eyes and a pointed gun. The woman was standing behind her husband. It was to her that he first addressed his pleas, but the man interrupted angrily. White men wanted to imprison his wife for the crime of having a disease which they themselves were responsible for, having brought it to the Islands. Why couldn't they at least let her die in what little peace and comfort her own husband could give her? There was no answer for him except the cold, uncomforting wisdom of statistics and science. For six long hours Damien sat trying to explain the necessity for the system of segregation. He talked with unabating fervor. The reason for his eloquence was not a belief in the merits of the leper colony but that he knew that if he failed in his arguments there were guns waiting in the valley below, guns that would probably blast life away from these two bewildered beings, this husband and wife who only asked to be left alone and together. He used this attachment as a further argument and promised that if they acceded to the law there would be no attempt at any punishment for their attempts at frustrating the authorities and that the husband would be allowed, unmolested, to accompany his wife to the settlement.

His persuasions were successful. At dusk that evening, just as the police, apprehensive for his safety, were making plans for an attack, they were surprised by the approach of the priest and the couple. Damien informed the officials of the conditions under which the natives had surrendered. It is to the credit of the police that they kept his promises. There was no attempt at any retribution or punishment and the husband was permitted to stay with his wife and join the melancholy contingent.

The lepers sailed and the more pleasant tasks of his

parish occupied the priest again. The taint of the disease had left the district and for most of his parishioners time soon eased the memories and poignancies of the lepers' departure, but it was not so with him. He could not, nor was it his desire to, forget the destiny that awaited the unfortunates at Molokai. His thoughts followed them across the sea, and prayers were said daily at his altar for their welfare.

CHAPTER V

He was not alone in the work of pioneering. Throughout the Islands other priests were toiling with the same fervor, with the same persistency, and in many cases with equal success. A Father Leonore had, at this time, completed a new church at Wailuku, on the Island of Maui. This parish was the scene of a large influx of laborers, brought there to work the rapidly growing sugar plantation. The Bishop, realizing the impression that a large and colorful ceremony would produce among them, made arrangements for a numerous array of parish priests to assist at the dedication.

Damien was one of those who received a letter of summons. Without waiting for the coastal steamer he took passage aboard a small sailing cutter. Although the trip was presumably to be of short duration it is a singular fact that he had a presentiment that there never would be a return to his parish. Of this feeling he wrote a few months later:

". . . I heard, as it were, an interior voice telling me that I should never again see my beloved neophytes nor my beautiful chapels. A sadness enveloped me when I took my last glance at my Christian district of Kohala . . ."

The consecration of Father Leonore's church was the most solemn and magnificent ceremony, lasting almost the entire day, ever seen on the island of Maui. In a setting naturally beautiful, the glittering vestments of the mitered Bishop made a brave appearance as he stalked in stately procession, sprinkling holy water in triple repetition at the newly erected walls, incensing the twelve crosses, followed by his priests in winding column, and preceded by the tall symbol of his religion that sparkled and snared in golden dazzle the brightness of the tropic sunshine. A group of younger missionaries, newly arrived from Europe, supplemented the surpliced splendor of the resident priests in this ceremony, enacted on ground which until recently had been the scene of pagan barbarisms.

Even at this moment of visible victory the missionary spirit of the Bishop was not appeased. After the rites he addressed his clergy, praising them for their progress, but also telling them of the problems that remained in the Vicariate. At such a discussion notorious Molokai could not be overlooked. When the Bishop spoke of the dread place his voice became gloomy. The history of the sad settlement was not without its record of missionary work, both Protestant and Catholic. Just a few months back a courageous lay worker* had erected a small wooden chapel; and in the past, three priests† had, at various times, relinquished their regular duties to make short stays; but such visits, before the strictness of the new Board of Health regulations, would have to cease. In the future any man that went to Molokai would have to remain there for the rest of his life. As the Bishop said this, his voice faltered. Even he could not demand such a sacrifice of anybody.

However, there was no need for him to voice a further appeal. No sooner were his words ended, than four priests, one of whom was Damien, sprang to their feet and pleaded to be allowed to live and work among the lepers.

The Superior's eyes dimmed with tears as he gazed at the four faces, each glowing with earnestness and sincerity. It was a hard decision to make. Even in modern times, with the advance of medicine and hygiene at its present efficiency, it would be a difficult problem. That day, on the island of Maui, the Vicar Apostolic was heavily burdened

* Brother Bertrand.

† Frs. Raymund, Albert and Boniface.

87

with the knowledge that the one he chose was certain to catch the horrible sickness. He looked at each of the four young countenances that were now so ardently turned to him, knowing well the one he picked would lose its fresh healthiness before the savage inroads of the incurable scourge.

Damien could see his superior's indecision. "My lord," he said, indicating his younger colleagues, "here are your new missioners. One of them could easily take my district. . . ." He pleaded that experience such as he already possessed would be needed at the settlement, and as he talked the Bishop remembered the record of courage and pioneering toil at Puno and Kohala. There could be no doubt but that this was the man for Molokai. The episcopal hand fell on Damien's shoulder.

"This employment," said Msgr. Maigret in a low voice and speaking with difficulty, as though conscious he was pronouncing a death sentence, "is of such a nature that I would not have imposed it on anyone, but I gladly accept your offer."

The affair was settled. Although everybody present knew that Damien had selected for himself a martyr's death, there were no attempts at speeches or laudations of any kind, save perhaps a few silent handclasps of farewell.

A steamer was waiting to take Bishop Maigret to Honolulu. It was decided that Damien should accompany him. Thus, one hour after the decision that had changed his life, the priest was once again on the sea which always, for him, was the prologue to new and unknown experience. On arrival in Honolulu harbor it was discovered that a batch of fifty lepers was being shipped that very evening to the colony. The opportunity could not have been more favorable to the priest. If he spent precious weeks making preparations for the exile, the authorities, not particularly well-disposed at this time to the Catholic clergy, might possibly find a pretext to prevent his going. It would be wise, he urged upon Msgr. Maigret, to let him sail immediately. Once again a sudden decision was arrived at. Without even time to purchase or collect any belongings other than one extra shirt and his breviary, the priest and his superior, who decided to remain with him until he reached Molokai, transferred to the other steamer just as the mooring lines were cast off.

The new ship, the inter-island steamer "Kilauea," was a vessel of despair. Groups of lepers, with pathetic bundles of belongings, huddled by the rails and waved their last goodbyes to the crowds on the wharf. All wore the usual flowers but instead of the happy chanting, customary to the departure of ships from Honolulu harbor, there was a strange dirge of sobbing and weeping and doleful singing which surged loud and ebbed to almost a whisper but never ceased. Damien's eyes could not resist roving from face to face. There were some with no apparent blemish. There were others, already marked with a hideousness that made him shudder.

The gangplank was lowered, the hawsers were cast off and as the breach widened between the ship and the wharf, a chorus of agonized cries rose high as the doomed and the ones that they were leaving gazed on each other for the last time. In fragrant clouds *leis* of flowers fluttered to the water in futile sad observance of an old custom which says that whoever, on leaving Honolulu, casts fresh blossoms upon the harbor waters is certain to return.

A herd of cattle was also being transported and their terrified bellowings mingled with the human weeping and sobbing that persisted throughout the long hours of the night as the vessel plunged on to its tragic destination. There could be no question of sleep for the Bishop or for Damien but they did not talk. They sat, each with his own thoughts, still and silent, on the deck mattresses that a kindly steward had placed for them in the lee of the chart room on the small upper deck.

In the dim chill hour that precedes dawn the ship fetched

up off the portion of the coast (Kalawao) where the lepers were to be landed. As there was no protected wharf a boat had to be lowered. The two priests clambered down the lurching flanks of the steamer into the life-boat and then, with other passengers, were rowed to the shore. It was dark, and a faint haze, adding to the dim veil of the hour, obscured the coast, making it difficult for Damien who peered through the grayness, anxious to glimpse the place where he was to spend the rest of his life.

From the sea the precipitous and jagged outlines of Molokai loom solemn and rather terrible. On that cold early morning, with the surf thundering high, the island must have seemed very unfriendly. Swinging lanterns flickered on the beach. As the ship's boat shot forward on the swell the occupants could see that a crowd had assembled to meet them.

There were lepers on board the ship and there had been lepers in his parish, but Damien had never seen the effects of the advanced stages of the disease until he set foot on that beach. The people who greeted him seemed to be but remnants of human beings, rotted and bloated beyond ordinary shape. Seeing his reaction to this horror, the understanding Bishop offered him a chance to change his mind, but the priest shook his head firmly and said his decision was just as firm as it had been at Maui. He was resolved to stay at Molokai.

The rest of the passengers were landed and the boat waited, ready to take back the Bishop who lingered in uneasy silence. It was a difficult moment for him. Although he had been prepared, he dreaded the final moment of parting; the leaving of the young priest on this unfriendly beach. His hesitation was broken by the coxswain of the boat shouting impatiently that he could not wait much longer. Unable to find words for Damien, the Bishop turned to the gaping lepers who surrounded them.

"So far, my children," he told them in their own language, "you have been left alone and uncared for. But you shall be so no longer. I have brought you one who will be a father to you, and who loves you so much that for your welfare and for the sake of your immortal souls, he does not hesitate to become one of you; to live and die with you."

He raised his hand in benediction and Damien fell to his knees with bared head. There were a few hasty words of farewell and in a profound silence the staring crowd watched the Bishop walk to the boat; that link with an outside world which for them had ceased to exist. Even the lowliest seaman of its crew, crouching over out-thrust oars, was in their eyes surrounded with glamour. The coxswain shouted a hoarse command, blades dipped in the swell. Damien, with a sense of great solitude settling around him, watched the boat become smaller until it reached the side of the steamer.

The sun was rising now but the mist prevented the usual golden splendor and the sea remained gray and dreary. Damien watched the ship. The boat was being hoisted on board. The protesting creak of the block and tackle could be heard. A white splotch of steam was suddenly born on the forecastle head and the harsh rattle of the windlass told that the anchor was being lifted. He could hear, as though it were a faint whisper from another planet, the shouted cry of the ship's officer who in the eyes of the bow scanned the anchor as it broke surface. He could see a small black figure raise an arm in a last salute.

There was a mournful hoot from the ship's whistle, the vessel turned and, with rigging etched against the pale morning light, headed toward the open sea.

Farewell, indeed it was for Damien.

CHAPTER VI

Death before death is what the ancient Egyptians called leprosy. It is a fit description. Down through the centuries it has been known as the most incurable, the most dreaded of diseases. The Hebrew scribes wrote of it with horror. Roman and Greek writings show that those races shared a similar fear. To-day, still baffling the ingenuities of modern science, it remains a scourge of mankind.

The valley of the Nile, that scene upon which the pageant of history has been so richly painted, seems to have also seen the origin of the hated malady. Fifty centuries ago, according to traditions preserved in the hieroglyphics of a later age, there was a severe plague of the disease and fourteen hundred years after this mention a sudden epidemic of it almost decimated the entire slave population of the Sudan. In 1375 B.C. Amenhotep IV, predecessor of Tutankhamen, tried to supplant the separate worshiping of the numerous divinities with a new creed that paid tribute only to the Sun God. But a united and outraged priesthood was able to defy and defeat the ruler by threatening a visitation of divine punishment in the form of a leprous curse to all who disobeyed them and followed the doctrines of the attempted monotheistic reform.

The waters that feed the fertile valley are blamed by some Egyptian historians for the disease. Many modern medical men agree that the conditions caused by the river (the warm, damp climate, the massed population, the continual fish diet, the yearly flooding of the marsh lands) presented excellent breeding grounds for the germ, although it must not be supposed that the disease is confined to these boundaries. Leprosy has been found in the cold climate of Iceland, in the mountainous parts of India, among the non-fish-eating tribes of Africa; and has flourished in the uncongested islands of the south Pacific.

Modern science has isolated the bacillus but an actual cure, or even a knowledge of its communicability, still bewilders the men of science; yet one of the first achievements recorded in the history of medicine was the perception of the transmissibility of leprosy by the Assyrio-Babylonians. There is frequent mention of it in the Bible and the Talmud; but because it seldom seems to have been regarded as absolutely incurable, many modern authorities declare that the ancient scribes classified any severe skin ailment as being a leprous taint.

The Hebrews had their physicians but the more serious ailments were regarded as an expression of the wrath of God and as such were left in the province of the priests whose only answer on such occasions was divine compassion sought by prayer. No earthly palliative was attempted once a man was infected, but by every means within their power those ancient rabbis tried to *prevent* the likelihood of any contagious disease; in fact, they were the founders of prophylaxis and in addition to their duties at the altar they acted as a species of medical police or health officers. Because of their careful inspection of meat for food, a thorough anatomical knowledge was acquired; in the time of David when he placed the Ark of the Covenant in Jerusalem and organized his armies the laws of sanitation and hygiene were observed with a strictness that would be creditable to any modern community. For inspiration the Jews had the wisdom of Moses who (in Deuteronomy) specified a most careful diet; and no martinet was ever more particular than he in the matter of policing camps and other similar elementary precautions for the safe-guarding of health. Rules for the prevention of leprosy and virulent sicknesses are carefully prescribed in the Book of Leviticus.

In the same work definite instructions are given in the advisability of disinfection and segregation.

This last means has been the only weapon that mankind, failing a cure or knowledge of cause, has ever been able to utilize to stem the inroads of leprosy. Therefore, throughout the ages and in all countries, the miseries of the leper have been made more acute because of the state of outlawry, worse than that shown to a criminal, thrust upon him.

It is not known with any degree of exactitude when leprosy first took root in Europe proper. (There is mention of it in India in 1400 B.C., in Persia, 800 B.C.) It is almost certain that it was not known until after the Romans had invaded Egypt. Soldiers and sailors have always been notorious carriers of disease and the Phœnician seamen are blamed by some for having carried leprosy to certain Mediterranean ports, while there are others who claim that the returning legions brought it to Rome. From Rome those same warriors marched north to Germany and by their side went the specter of the scourge.

By 550 A.D. the pestilence had even taken foothold in far away Ireland. Not so long after that, it had spread so rapidly that leper hospitals were being opened in England. It gradually increased in that country up to the time of the Crusades when it suddenly took on the proportions of an enormous and devastating plague. Quite erroneously the Crusaders have been blamed for the *introduction* of the disease into northern Europe; this is not true, but there is no doubt that they brought back enough of the deadly germs to start the formidable epidemics which occurred simultaneously with their return.

During the twelfth and thirteenth centuries the ravages of the plague assumed monstrous proportions. It is estimated that at one period at least a quarter of northern Europe's population were lepers. England was the most sorely affected, for there the disease met a rich soil in which to flourish. Personal sanitation and cleanliness were in a lamentable state, the towns were congested, filthy, and without any drainage facilities, and the diet of the majority of the burghers seemed to have consisted of a species of black bread, salted meats, and fishes that were putrid rather than preserved. Most of the population passed their entire lives without tasting a vegetable of any kind and rare was the man who bothered to change his daytime attire for bed and slumber. The common sense laws of hygiene as preached by the ancient Hebrews had been abandoned but there were still some biblical injunctions remembered.

"And the leper in whom the plague is, his clothes shall be rent, and the hair of his head shall go loose, and he shall cover his upper lip, and shall cry unclean, unclean. All the days wherein the plague is in him he shall be unclean; he is unclean; he shall dwell alone; without the camp shall his dwelling be." (Leviticus XIII, 45)

"Unclean!" The tragic cry echoed throughout the land as the afflicted were cast from cities and bidden to exist as best they could. Further decrees were issued to harass them.

"The leper must not go about without his black cowl."
"He must not enter churches, mills or bakeries."
"He must not come to fairs or markets."
"He must not wash face or hands at public drinking fountains."
"He must not touch anything except with his stick."
"He must not answer if spoken to until he who speaks to him is to windward of him."
"He must not walk along narrow ways at evening-tide."
"He must not live in town or village."
"His only dwelling must be in the open country far from men and the roads."

A leper was regarded as being already dead; the burial service was read over him, and his properties were given to his heirs. The corpse-like putrefaction of his flesh and quotations from the Old Testament were some of the reasons upon which this treatment was justified, but before it was applied the greatest care was taken to make sure that the suspect had actual leprosy. With great ceremony his person and his history was examined meticulously; for upon the physicians' judgment rested the heavy responsibility of isolating him from his family and his possessions. After the diagnosis a medical certificate would be solemnly posted for all to see, declaring that he was either healthy or a leper before God and man. If it were the latter case the document would be worded similarly to the following statement:

"We, sworn physicians, have examined this man by order of the authorities, to disclose if he be leprous. We report as follows:

"We have found, particularly, his face to be pimply and of a violet color. We pulled a hair from his beard and another from his eyebrow, and at the root of each hair a minute fragment of flesh was attached. We found small tubercles around the eyebrows and behind the ears. The expression is fixed and immobile. The breath is evil, and the voice hoarse and nasal. . . . From these and other unmistakable signs we solemnly declare that he is a leper."

The unfortunate one was then turned over to the ecclesiastical authorities who usually arrived shortly after midnight to remind him that his plight was a punishment from God and that there could be no escape. He was sprinkled with holy water and then, in solemn procession, led by cross bearer and priest, taken to the church where all the somber arrangements of a Requiem Mass awaited. With that resignation to circumstances that comes so easy to human nature his friends and family would be assembled, dressed in mourning attire, shedding tears of grief, but already considering him irretrievably lost to this world as though he were an actual corpse. From this moment he would be but a memory to them; pious prayers might be offered for the repose of his soul but little would be done for his body. The church services were the same as though he were deceased, except that, instead of a bier, a canopy of black cloth was erected near the altar and in its dark shadow the leper was placed.

Nor did the grisly performance end with the Mass but was continued to the graveyard, where beside a freshly dug pit the leper again knelt while the officiating priest threw a handful of earth over him as a final sign that in the eyes of his fellowmen he was dead; and even though there were breath in his unfortunate body, that body was henceforth doomed to the boundaries of the grave. The scanty possessions of his banishment were then given to him: a black cowl, a wicker basket, special gloves, a barrel and a long stick upon which there was a rattle.

"You are given this rattle," he was told, "to warn men of your unclean presence." And at the sound of the rattle people would make the sign of the cross and flee; or the more cruel might seize stones and drive the luckless outcast to a different direction.

As the plague assumed its larger proportions these harsh laws became impracticable because of the vast numbers of those affected. Lepers were everywhere. The nobles and the rich could care for themselves, but among the poorer classes the problem became a menace which threatened to engulf and overwhelm the entire race.

It was the Church that finally came to the rescue. Much has been written and said to the detriment of the clergy of medieval times; there have been accusations of laxity in conduct, and stories have been told of the amassing of wealth by the monasteries, but the fact remains that it was through the brave and unceasing labors of the priesthood that leprosy was finally stamped out in Europe. At a date when the ominous sound of a leper's rattle sent most men scurrying, the early monks rallied together and converted their houses into leper hospitals and lazar houses. In France, during the thirteenth century, it is recorded that no less than *two thousand* of these institutions existed and in England at the same period there were two hundred founded, of which the majority were controlled by the ecclesiastics.

"All guests who come shall be received as though they were Christ" was the rule of the lazar houses and it was a rule that was faithfully observed. Nobody, in those times of famine and pestilence, cruelty and persecution, was ever turned away and the same hearty welcome and treatment was accorded to all, regardless of rank. Naturally there was a heavy burden of expense; to procure funds the Abbots and the Bishops enlisted the support of the nobles. Tolls and tithes were levied, fairs were held, and legacies encouraged. Chivalrous orders, such as the Knights of Lazarus and the Knights of St. John of Jerusalem, were inspired to help the work of the monks in supervising and caring for the inmates of the leper hospitals. Henry III displayed a surprising generosity, endowing hospitals and making lavish gifts to the Abbots, although he was pleading poverty and begging Pope Alexander IV for an extension of time for certain debts owed to Rome.

Each lazar house had its own rules, which varied greatly according to the community. Gallows were erected at the gate of one establishment as a warning to the inmates of what they might expect if they attempted to leave monastery boundaries, whereas at another house the penalty for any infringement of discipline was instant expulsion to the outer world. Nevertheless, despite the lack of uniform regulations, the lazar houses were tremendously successful and must be recognized as such. For the first time in history consideration was shown the leper; he was well-fed; (a loaf of bread and a gallon of ale was the daily ration to a patient in one hospital, along with a weekly supply of cheese, meat and fish); he was sufficiently clothed, a roof was over his head and his spiritual needs were attended. There are extant many old churches of medieval architecture that still possess what is known as the "leper window." This is a low opening, often barred and shuttered, cut in the chancel wall; and through it in ancient times the lepers, gathered in the churchyard, could peer and thus attend Mass, for they were allowed after the eighth century to receive Holy Communion, a privilege given to them by the liberal pontiff, Gregory II.

Leprosy was not the only epidemic disease of the Middle Ages; the dreadful squalor, the bad sanitation, the gross immorality, the continual migration of vagabond characters, were all conducive to the rapid spread of such sicknesses as typhus, cholera, influenza, scabies, syphilis and the Black Plague. The last named was the most formidable, coming after and succeeding the tides of leprosy. Other maladies had given slow and lingering agonies, but this new one caused a direct and sudden mortality of one fourth of the population of the known world, bringing panic and confusion to a dismayed humanity that thought it already had experienced the worst of diseases. The doors of the lazar houses were opened to the sufferers of this new scourge; indeed it was found that the leper, already weakened with the burden of his own sickness, usually was the first to contract the plague. *Mortalega grande* (the great mortality) is what the Italians called this latest terror, and it was well named for he who got it was sure to die swiftly; and twenty-five thousand of the clergy in England alone are declared to have succumbed before it. The dead were hurled into hastily dug pits and even this slight precaution ceased as the roll of deaths mounted higher; soon putrefying corpses lay unheeded in street and house. But even the Black Plague was not without one good effect, for when the epidemic had subsided, (as quickly as it had come) it was found the ranks of the lepers had suffered the most. Those that remained were kept carefully quarantined in the lazar houses, and the result was that by 1346 there was not a leper left in London. The rapid decline of the disease continued, and, although for a while it persisted in Scotland, it had ceased in Europe, except for a few isolated cases, by the end of the fifteenth century.

Medicine was not the advanced and respected science then that it is now. The first medical book to be printed in England was *"A Passing Gode Lityll Boke Necessarye and Behovefull Agenst the Pestilence,"* * a small quarto of twelve leaves translated from the Latin of the papal physician, Jean Jasme. Dependable drugs and surgical instruments were almost as sparse as medical bibliography. Physicians, except for a few outstanding pioneers who came in the fifteenth century, Paracelsus, Vesalius and Pare, were for the most part either misguided pseudo-scholars who made a great show of their learning and took their theories from early Latin writings or were strolling quacks who learned their trade from barbers, gypsies, undertakers, fortune-tellers and midwives.

With a leper, tradition bound the physician to consider his task completed with the diagnosis and recognition of the disease, for even if he had been willing it was considered that a mere mortal should not dare to meddle with what was so obviously a punishment sent by God. In the lazar houses the monks cared for the lepers, giving them some degree of solace and comfort, even dressing their sores, but there was never any attempt at any treatment by the physicians.

The seventeenth century brought brilliant men. It was the age of Shakespeare, Milton and Cervantes, Bacon, Newton, Rembrandt, Raleigh, Wren and scores of others whose names stand for genius or great talent. The universities of Bologna, Padua, and Pisa, along with those of Paris and Montpellier and many new institutions of learning, were turning out students well versed in a knowledge of medicine. The status of the medical profession, freed from quackery and herb-doctoring, reached higher levels. There

* Printed in London by William de Machlinia in the year 1480.

were physicians such as Gilbert and Harvey of England; there was the learned Jesuit Athanasius Kircher, who was mathematician, musician, physicist and optician; there was the great microscopist, Anton van Leeuwenhoek; the versatile physician-priest, Niels Adensen of Copenhagen, whose conversion from Lutherism to Catholicism is one of the most romantic episodes of human history; there were Malpighi and Francesco Redi and a list of other names equally illustrious which could continue for pages.

But with all this learning, with the rise of such individual brilliance, it is a strange fact that the administration of hospitals slumped to a lower standard than that of the preceding centuries. With the extermination of the medieval plague most of the lazar houses had been shut, but the ones that remained in existence had been turned over to the civil authorities to become, eventually, pestholes of extraordinary filthiness where the nursing and feeding of the sick were of a haphazard nature. Incredible as it may seem, these conditions were no temporary state of affairs; the science of medicine continued to advance but it is shameful history that there was little improvement among hospitals until the middle of the nineteenth century. Until then a hospital, in most cases, was known as an undesirable and gloomy place of unsavory repute, a place where the poor were put and left to die.

Careful nursing and peaceful surroundings are the only solaces that can ease the existence of lepers but from the fifteenth century to Damien's time there was no progress in their welfare; indeed, during those centuries a sufferer from the dread malady might be said to be in a far worse position than the lepers of earlier times. Time had taught that isolation of the diseased was necessary, and as has been seen, the epidemics of the Middle Ages had been met with the open doors of the hospitable lazar houses. But when the sufferers became few and remote, and usually of the poorer classes and at some distant outpost of the white man's venturings, the sentence of segregation meant a grim life-imprisonment in a hopeless place that even in the days of fantastic penal punishments would have sufficed to make the most jail-hardened prisoner shudder. It would need the pen of a Dante to describe the hardships and cruelties of those squalid prisons where forgotten creatures, already doomed to die the most frightful of deaths, were begrudged the life that persisted in their miserable bodies. Objects of repulsion, feared by all, they were not wanted on this earth and in every way were shown that the sooner their actual death occurred the better it would be for humanity.

Such was the shocking state of the majority of the world's leper institutions when on that dismal morning of May, 1873, the Belgian priest landed on the surf-beaten beach that fringed the most appalling of them all: the notorious Kalawao settlement on the gray island of Molokai.

CHAPTER VII

He was alone and he felt his loneliness. It was hard to feel any kinship with the live things that crowded about him. They were without faces or if they had faces they were distorted beyond resemblance to any human shape. Where eyes had been there were craters of pus; and there were gaping cavities, disease-infected holes, that merged with rotting mouths, where noses should be. Ears were pendulous masses many times their natural size, or were shriveled to almost nothing. Hands were without fingers and some arms were merely stumps. Feet and legs were equally repulsive and the bodies of most of these wretched creatures were bloated and pitted, shrunken and swollen, but never of a normal shape. They were a pitiable, revolting sight; their wounds and sores being either entirely undressed or covered with filthy matter-soaked rags.

There were a few whom the ravages of the disease had not yet blemished to a perceptible degree, but Damien did not see them; his eyes, unwilling, but fascinated, clung to the horrors, for in them he saw his own eventual fate. He thought that surely those creatures must be the most sorely affected, those in the last stages of disease; but he was wrong, the worst cases he was yet to see, for they were too crippled to walk the three rocky miles that separated their miserable quarters from the ocean.

Several years later, Robert Louis Stevenson was to visit the colony. Much better conditions existed then because of Damien's work; there was order and reform but even so the author recoiled from

". . . an ordeal from which the nerves of a man's spirit shrink, even as his eye quails under the light of the sun. . . . A pitiful place to visit and a hell to dwell in. . . . I am not a man more than usually timid, but I never recall the days and nights I spent upon that island promontory (eight days and seven nights) without heartfelt thankfulness that I am somewhere else. . . ."

As for the inhabitants of that place he was shocked into writing that they resembled:

"Gorgons and Chimaeras dire . . . pantomime deformations of our common manhood. Such a population as only now and again surrounds us in the horrors of a nightmare."

Flanked by such a group the priest was escorted to the assortment of makeshift huts which, huddled together in wretched squalor, was called by courtesy a village. As in any other native village there were women and children sitting in front of their abodes but there was a grim difference here; the women that Damien saw were not laughing or gossiping or engaged in busy domestic tasks. They sat still and listless, although not too listless to avert their ravaged faces, as though in shame, as the white man passed. The children seemed equally apathetic, squatting like dwarfed old men with unchildlike solemnity. Those of them who were infected with the disease looked, with their swollen heads and frail bodies, like the reflections of pitiful gnomes seen in a concave mirror.

The huts were primitive affairs, affording little shelter, and made for the most part of untrimmed boughs and branches leaned together and roughly thatched with long grass. There were remains of more permanent dwellings in the shape of a few ruined stone walls; in their unroofed shadows dwelt entire families with only filthy mats to shelter them from the inclemencies of the weather.

Not a corner of the dreadful place did Damien leave unvisited on that day of his arrival. He tramped everywhere, his heart aching at the pitiful misery that confronted him on all sides. Almost as depressing as the visible effects of the disease was the air of hopelessness and fear that permeated the entire settlement. The words that Dante saw written above the gates of hell could well fit this community: "All hope abandon, ye who enter here!" And the very scenery seemed to match the forbidding spirit of the place; the formidable walls of rock that towered to the sky, shutting off the promontory from the rest of the island, were like the barriers of a weird and gigantic prison; and the tall black rocks of lava that jutted from the sparse vegetation were like twisted tombstones in a huge abandoned graveyard. The plaintive cries of the wheeling birds and the ceaseless booming of the surf served to complete the funereal note.

In those depressing surroundings Damien found one sign of a better influence in the shape of a small wooden chapel. To him, who was so full of faith, it must have been a welcome moment when he stepped across the threshold. It was tiny, it was of the rudest construction, and it plainly showed a lack of care, but it was a house dedicated to the worship of his God: the Supreme Being in whose service he had ventured to the island. He knelt before the altar in prayer, but not for long. Ever practical he soon rose and improvising a broom from the branches of a nearby tree he commenced his first work on Molokai, the cleaning of the chapel of St. Philomena.

A Catholic leper brought fruit, timidly offering it to the priest for his midday meal. Damien took the gift from the diseased hands without showing any emotion other than gratefulness; from the beginning he was resolved to show the lepers that he experienced no fear or repulsion of them or their affliction. Another leper brought flowers, and soon the church was fragrant with the smell of orange blossoms and cheerful with sprays of yellow hibiscus and white poppy. It took him four hours to clean the church interior and in that time the ring of watchers that had formed at the door took on the proportions of a crowd. To them it was a novel sight to see a white man toiling on his knees, a non-leper who did not recoil when they approached.

As yet he had made no provision for his own lodging nor was he to have much time to spend on such a (to him) trivial matter. No sooner were his labors in the church completed than he was asked to officiate at the burial of a leper who had died the preceding day.

Death was too frequent a happening among those doomed people to cause any undue interest. Not a day passed without at least one poor wretch being freed of his earthly miseries, and the funeral "ceremony" meant merely the disposing of his remains with the least amount of trouble. There was no coffin to hold the corpse over which Damien read the words of his first burial service at Molokai. The body was wrapped in pieces of old matting. There was no hearse, or, indeed, vehicle of any kind, to transport it to the final resting place. The grisly burden in its inadequate shroud was awkwardly carried on the shoulders of four lepers who themselves expected a similar favor in the not distant future. (At that time the average life-span of a leper after being landed at Molokai was estimated at being between three and four years.)

The priest was shocked when he found that the grave was but a shallow ditch, hastily scooped to a depth just sufficient to receive the corpse. There had been rains the day before and the fenceless cemetery was thick with mud, but in the sea of slime he could see that recent graves had been disturbed; there was a dreadful litter of exposed bones and a sickening stench like that of a battlefield from which the living troops have long passed. Damien was further shocked when one of the pallbearers informed him that at night packs of wild dogs and swine prowled the grave-yard, feeding on what they could find. He read the words of the burial service, but as he closed his missal his mind was already busy with plans. Not that he had long to reflect; as he walked back to the village his arm was plucked at by an old woman who though untouched by leprosy was shriveled and broken with age. She was not a Catholic, she told him, but her son was, and he was dying. Would the priest come?

It was a foul inclosure she led him to, a hovel with an interior so filthy that Damien in the ensuing hours was forced to leave several times in order to breathe the purer air. The rain had soaked through the inadequate roof and, as at the graveyard, he found his feet were ankle deep in mud. By the dim light he could see the dying man prostrate on an unpleasant mess of rush mats that were soggy with his own filth. Overcoming a mounting nausea by sheer will-power, the priest knelt down to give his greeting to the invalid who was conscious, although so decayed by the disease that he seemed to be but a shapeless mass of decomposed flesh. The dying leper was glad to see the white man, for he had kept his faith and was indeed a devout Catholic. There were only two fingers remaining on his right hand but he still managed to clasp, with extraordinary devotion, the tattered leaves of a coverless and stained prayer book. In a voice that was just the echo of a hoarse whisper, he bade his mother to remain quiet, for she was moaning her misery as the priest made his arrangements for the last rite of the Church—the Sacrament which was instituted by Jesus Christ and in which the dying receive, by the anointing of the oil and the prayers of the priest, that consolation which comes with the grace of God.

Damien went about his task. With the holy oil he anointed the sore-infested ears of the leper, then the eyes, the nose, and, as prescribed by the rites of the Church, he then turned to the leper's feet, there to be confronted with a horror that made even him hesitate. There was no power in any of the leper's limbs, in fact he was paralyzed in what remained of both legs, yet the feet were *moving*. To use Damien's own words: ". . . I discovered his foot was being gnawed away by the worms." Putrefaction had already set in and the priest was to find it was to become a familiar and to be expected experience whenever it was his gruesome duty to administer Extreme Unction to a leper. The preceding quotation is from a letter, written three weeks after his arrival, in which he was describing the death of yet another man.

Daylight had vanished entirely when, to the accompaniment of piteous cries from the crone, her son's eyes flickered and shut for the last time. Damien recited the litany of the dying and remained, his lips moving in continual prayer, half an hour by the side of the dreadful corpse. Then he persuaded the woman to leave the hut. It must have given him, to whom it meant so much, a great satisfaction when, as he bade her farewell for the night, she asked him if he would receive her into the Church. Now that her son had gone she felt no longer any need to live; she had seen the peace that the priest's religion had brought to the deathbed; and she wanted some of that same solace and tranquillity at her own end which she, with the premonition and power to will their own death so peculiar to the ancient Polynesians, was certain would come soon. Damien baptized her the next day; she died two hours later, to be buried, as she wished, alongside the body of her son.

The first night on the island, and for many nights after, he made his bed on the bare ground beneath the scanty shelter of the overflowing branches of a large *pandanus* tree that grew near the chapel. Fortunately, there was no rain on that first occasion. Even so, the tangled roots which gave house to a world of innumerable ants, scorpions and mosquitoes must have proven an extremely uncomfortable couch. But even had it been a feather mattress in the most secure of shelters, it is doubtful whether slumber could have brought a happy, if temporary, forgetfulness of the things he had seen during the day.

He said his prayers, "lit a pipe and leaned against the tree trunk, thinking. . . ." He leaves no record of what those thoughts were, but we know this was the first time he had for uninterrupted meditation since his arrival. The night and a cloud-covered sky had effaced most of the visible horrors with a darkness, impenetrable and stifling; occasionally there would be the rustle of leaves, and he would be startled by a glimpse of an appallingly scarred face staring at him. He would speak and it would vanish as quickly as it had come. The busy activity of the day might have served to numb the solitude he felt on the beach in the morning but the inactivity of the night must have brought back that feeling with a tenfold acuteness. There must have been thoughts of the tranquillity of Tremeloo, the happy enthusiasms of seminary days, the comparative contentment that had been his at Puno and Kohola.

But inevitable as memories are he was not the man to waste time in regrets. One thing is certain of those long night hours—his mind, the fountain of his almost incredible energy, must have been teeming with plans. There was much to do at Molokai, a task so vast and with a complexity of difficulties so disheartening that to any ordinary man a beginning, without aid of any kind of power or authority, would have seemed futile. Even with a corps of doctors, engineers and police the work would have been tremendous. Damien had none of these things. He did have what he considered more important: he had faith, a belief that divine assistance was there to help him. And when he prayed it was an appeal for strength to continue at his duty, for a duty he always considered it to be. Never by a single act or word of condescension was he to show that he regarded his services or coming to Molokai as a deed particularly heroic or a favor in any way to the lepers. Sore-scarred faces and limbless bodies were a perpetual reminder to him that it was the men of his own race who were responsible for the introduction of the terrible scourge to the Islanders.

The night did not pass in silence. There were sounds from the village that failed to lessen as the hours passed; there were the usual plaints, sudden and occasional, from the sorely ill; there were demoniac cries from those whom the disease had driven insane and there was the gibbering of an idiot child. There were other sounds, too, that finally made him stand to his feet, listening to what seemed impossible in these unhappy surroundings; drunken shouts and wild outbursts of laughter that unmistakably told of a carousal being held in one of the huts. But such debauches were not unusual and he was to discover that the morals of the colony were as unhealthy and viciously bad as they could be. The place had its women of easy virtue (in some of its phases it is a strange fact that leprosy has a strong aphrodisiacal effect) who plied their trade among public scenes of unleashed sensual licence. There were illicit distillers who concocted a fiery and strong species of intoxicating liquor. There were cardsharps and other varieties of criminals. Of these conditions the priest made report that:

". . . vice reigned instead of virtue. When new lepers came, the old ones were eager to impress them with the principle: *aole kanawai ma keia wahi*—'In this place is no law.' I was obliged to fight against such defiance of Divine as well as human laws. . . . Under primitive roofs they lived in the most revolting promiscuity, without distinction of age or sex, old or new cases, all more or less strangers to one another, these unfortunate outcasts of society. . . . Many an unfortunate woman had had to become a prostitute in order to win care for her children. When she was attacked by the disease, she and her children were cast out and had to find another shelter; sometimes they were thrust behind a stone wall and left there to die, or they were carried to the hospital and deserted.

"Another source of immorality was intemperance. There grows along the side of the mountains a plant that the natives call Ki, whose root when fermented and distilled yields a highly intoxicating liquor which, owing to the crude and imperfect distilling process, is unfit for drinking. The distilling of this liquor was being carried on to a horrible extent when I arrived, and its consequences can be more easily imagined than described on paper. Under its influence the natives would abandon all decency and run about naked and acting as though mad. I went around, and at last, by threats and persuasion, got the natives to give up their stills. . . . But for a long time they neglected everything except prostitution and drinking."

In addition to a prodigious capacity for manual labor he was possessed of other qualities that now had the opportunity for full development. His flair for leadership and his executive ability succeeded in bringing discipline and order to the settlement for the first time, something that the Government with all the threats of armed forces had been unable to do. The lepers, apart from the Catholics, had greeted his arrival with either a sullen apathy or an active resentment. He was of a race which they rightly blamed not only for their disease but also for the laws of banishment to Molokai, and when he started to campaign against the régime of vice he was met with open resistance. There were many stormy clashes between him and the more debased characters. Violence was threatened several times, but his physical strength matched his courage. He made it quite plain that he had no fear of any man, not even a leper whose method of attack was to rush and embrace his opponent with arms and hands that were covered with open sores. Such threats had proved sufficient in the past to discourage any attempts at reform on the part of authority, but the priest was a man of different caliber.

From the beginning he realized that in order to win the respect and confidence of the settlement inmates it would be necessary to show absolutely no fear or repulsion at their disease. Rather than take pains to avoid contact with an infected person he deliberately made it a point to eat from the same dishes when sharing their humble meals and often his pipe was lent to a leper. Such methods to-day would be

111

called foolhardy; but it must be remembered that he was alone in that pesthole and that the only way to help the lepers was to get them interested enough to help themselves. The first steps in this direction would be for them to lose the suspicion and distrust with which bitter experience had taught them to regard a white man.

The *pandanus* tree continued to remain his shelter for several weeks as he was far too busy to seek or make a better residence. His hours were long, and the sky was still somber with night darkness when he was stirring in the early mornings. With shovel and ax he worked on the burial ground until the awful state was rectified. He dug graves that were at least six feet deep; with nothing but a few borrowed tools that were both old and crude he constructed coffins for which there was a daily demand. It is estimated that until better arrangements were made he constructed at least two thousand of these with his own hands. There was no doctor at the colony, and he made it part of his daily routine to visit the bedridden cases and change their bandages and wash their sores. The filthy state of the huts and the lamentable sanitation worried him.

"Nearly all were prostrated on the beds, in damp grass huts, their constitutions badly broken down. The smell of their filth, mixed with the exhalation of their sores, was simply disgusting, unbearable for a newcomer. Many times at their domiciles I have been compelled to run outside to breathe fresh air. . . ."

He was a confirmed pipe lover now and loyally adds . . . "on many occasions the smell of my pipe was my preservation, and saved me from carrying in my clothes the noxious odors."

He saw that the inadequate water supply was responsible for many of the bad conditions. Water had to be carried, usually in discarded old tins and bottles, from a gulch which was so distant that it was possible for the more helpless of the lepers to procure the precious fluid only by begging from their abler companions. Sometimes it was so scarce that many unfortunates actually suffered from thirst and never was there any water "wasted" on the cleansing of houses or the laundering of bandages and apparel.

Reasoning that where there were tall hills there must be mountain streams and perhaps springs, he made many inquiries and finally set out on a tour of exploration. At the end of a valley called Waihanau he found, much to his joy, what seemed to be a natural reservoir; a circular pool filled with delicious ice-cold water. It was a full seventy-five feet in diameter and a sounding revealed it to be eighteen feet deep, too large for any drought to dry.

There existed a "Superintendent" of the colony, a purely titular position held by a leper and native who, although he seemed to be a well-meaning man, received scant attention from both the authorities in Honolulu and his fellow lepers. To him Damien went and demanded that a petition be sent to the Government asking for a supply of piping, medical supplies, building equipment and a doctor. Of course this petition was ignored, but the priest persisted, pestering the agent into writing a continual flow of letters and himself bombarding the Board of Health with a relentless barrage of reports and complaints.

The first results of this persistence came in the shape of a cargo of water pipes brought aboard the schooner "Warwick." No engineer or artisan came with this welcome freight, but Damien, with a vision of an adequate water supply before him, did not care. From hut to hut he canvassed, seeking men sufficiently fit to help him carry the pipes and put them into position. At first he found it extremely hard to find such volunteers. Those people came of a race naturally indolent and were possessed of an ailment that made them even more languid; then, too, they had the inertia of despair.

The priest, however, was not to be refused; he sought to convey his enthusiasm with long speeches and he cajoled. As the Hawaiians are notoriously susceptible to oratory, he finally shamed them into mustering a small working crew. These he marched to the beach landing where the schooner's sailors were unloading the piping. The seamen, true specimens of their calling, were men of brawn and the priest, gauging their muscles with a shrewd and appraising eye, conceived an idea. Turning to their captain* he made him the victim of a harangue in which his sense of chivalry, nobility of character and generosity of heart were successively and rapidly appealed to. The mariner good-naturedly succumbed. Soon a gang of sailors, complete with the welcome aids of block and tackle equipment, were assisting the lepers in hauling the iron pipes into position, while the priest and the captain, using the sand on the beach as a drawing table, outlined the crude plans for the new water system.

After these were completed Damien rushed off to supervise; indeed he put the pipes in position with his own hands. There were many problems of topography and his only blueprint was the memory of the hasty sand-sketching but, after many days of herculean work, a steady stream of cold clear water pouring into the village told that the new system was successful. Taps were placed at close distances within reach of every hut and the lepers were astonished to find they had as much water as they needed, not only for drinking but for domestic purposes as well. The long weary pilgrimages to the distant springs suddenly ceased before this miracle of the faucet; and grateful eyes, alight with a new respect, were turned on this man whose pity for them had so strongly practical a bent.

There was, however, no resting on any laurels. The daily stint of grave-digging, coffin-making, doctoring and

* A native Hawaiian who had been trained in English ships and as a result bore the very Anglican name of John Bull.

a multitude of other miscellaneous labors, continued to keep him feverishly busy. His prestige might be increasing amongst the lepers but so was his discontent with the settlement's conditions. Eighty per cent of the lepers were desperately ill but this percentage could be substantially decreased if a higher standard of living could be brought about. The filthiness of the huts was an affront to his sense of decency, and as he brooded on ways and means of replacing them Nature came to his assistance with a heavy windstorm that really was a blessing in disguise for it completely wrecked the wretched shacks to a state beyond repair. Fragile walls were blown away and the pouring rains that followed washed the sites clean. It is true that the miserable inmates were left drenched to the skin and devoid of any sheltering, but after providing temporary relief by carrying the helpless to the uncertain but cleaner covering provided by the larger trees, Damien was actually happy. Now he had the basis for an appeal which he was quite sure the Government could not resist.

He penned a lengthy letter, stressing the immediate need for assistance and succor, and it so happened that just as he concluded the writing of this appeal, the schooner "Warwick" again dropped anchor off Kalawao. Damien procured a canoe and taking his letter paddled hastily to the vessel. As Captain Bull assisted him to the narrow poop he described graphically the deplorable plight of the settlement and begged the captain to report the same personally to the authorities upon his arrival in Honolulu.

"Why not come yourself?" Bull replied. "Your word would mean much more than mine." It was a sensible proposal, for Honolulu was actually but a short distance from Molokai, and at the most Damien need not be away from the settlement more than a few days. In that short time he probably could enlist help from many sources. Plans began to form in his head as he made a quick affirmative decision; he would ask the aid of the Bishop and the Mother Superior of the sisters, perhaps a committee of helpers might be organized among the more charitable of the town's citizens. Captain Bull lost no time in getting under way and soon the schooner, with help of a fair wind, was furrowing a rapid passage to Honolulu.

The priest must have inhaled the cool clean sea breeze gratefully as he watched the glimmers of the passing water, for it was a most welcome change from the stifling squalor of his late surroundings. The "Warwick" was no brass-mounted and teak-varnished yacht; she had been built strictly for utilitarian purposes, broad-beamed and deep-hulled for her length. Like all island schooners she had an air of jauntiness that was not alone due to her white paint and wings of canvas. Similar vessels still ply their trade among the less frequented islands of the South Seas and their arrival in those distant lagoons is much more of an event than the entry of a large liner into more civilized parts. Too small to have more than one tiny cabin their decks are usually a litter of colorful deck passengers, happy and pleasantly noisy. The captains are personages whose advice is sought on all matters; although a knowledge of a sextant is rather vague among these navigators, their skill is formidable when it comes to sliding through a reef crevice on the blackest of nights where the only warnings of dangerous proximities are the echoes of surf boomings and an instinct that cannot be gleaned from books.

The peaceful sea interlude did not last long for the priest. The next day, within an hour after the schooner's mooring lines had hurtled ashore, he was at the Bishop's residence. There, in the cool shadows of a wide vine-covered verandah, he explained his needs and plans to the sympathetic prelate who promised definite and quick material aid.

A far different reception awaited him at the offices of the Board of Health. He had had correspondence with those high-handed officials, but this was the first time he was to meet any of them. The moment he entered the door and gave his name to the nearest desk it was, of course, known who he was, and by every procrastinating device known to petty clerks and menials it was endeavored to show him how unimportant both he and his mission were. He was made to write and rewrite his name and the purpose of his visit. He was left, seemingly forgotten, for hours in a small and stuffy waiting room. Jealousy and a fear that his work was a reflection on their administration was probably the reason for this humiliating treatment. His voluntary exile had been a too heroic act to have been left unnoticed by the local newspapers and soon after his departure to Molokai there had appeared a glowing article * which among other things said: "Without bias in favour of the teaching which this man professes, we proclaim it aloud: He is a hero!"

When the President of the Board of Health finally condescended to receive Damien he made it quite obvious that he did not share this opinion but actually regarded him as an officious busybody who had overstepped the boundaries of his position as a missionary. With ill-concealed hostility he listened while the priest told of the dire need for necessities, then, impatiently interrupting, he declared that these things should not concern one whose province began and ended with the *spiritual* cares of the *Catholics* at Molokai

Damien looked at the well-fed President, comfortably ensconced behind the polished desk; beyond the well-tailored shoulders his eyes held the ineradicable vision of Molokai, and as the petulant complaint went on, he remembered the scenes that he had left only the preceding morning. Losing his temper, he minced no words as to what he thought of the Board of Health and its methods.

"You seem to forget, Father Damien," replied the official, his voice shaking with fury, "that there is a law which forbids anyone from the leper settlement to leave its boundaries."

* *Advertiser of Hawaii,* May 17, 1873.

"I am not a leper," said Damien.

"You live in the settlement and your presence here is a violation of the law. I suppose you are returning to Molokai but I warn you if ever you appear here again or even so much as cross the mountains that separate the leper colony from the rest of the island you shall be arrested and gaoled like any other felon!"

"There are times when it is imperative I should see my Bishop," answered Damien firmly, "and there are parishioners outside the settlement whom I shall have to visit."

The president's only reply was to walk abruptly out of the room without uttering another word. A few days later he sent an official letter to the priest, reiterating his threats. Damien answered in a short but firm note, saying that whenever the interests of the lepers or of his parishioners demanded it he would leave the settlement, despite any unjust measures that might follow.

A manifesto was then issued from the Board of Health to the effect that in future only lepers destined for the colony were to be allowed to land from the steamers and that nobody from the settlement was to be permitted to set foot on, or have contact in any way with, a ship that might be anchored off the shore. Captains were instructed rigidly to enforce this law among their passengers and crews and were told that, when necessity demanded the unloading of cargo, it was to be dumped into open boats or on an isolated part of the coast.

Almost to his death Damien was to continue quarreling with the authorities. Sometimes there might be brief periods of armistice but he was never to understand the slowness of Government methods. Living, as he did, amongst the sufferings of the wretched lepers, he could not but be exasperated when confronted with the delays and inefficiencies of official procedure and red tape. He was called "obstinate, headstrong, brusque, and officious" and undoubtedly he was all those things but the conditions he met needed an aggressiveness of an extraordinary de-

118

gree. A more pleasant or more tactful man would probably have despaired at the oppositions that sometimes confronted him. Government procrastination only served to make him

"vehement and excitable in regard to matters that did not seem to him right [wrote Joseph Dutton who was to be his assistant in later days], and he sometimes said and did things which he afterward regretted . . . but in all the differences he had a true desire to do right, to bring about what he thought was best. No doubt he erred sometimes in judgment, as all of us do. These things make his relations with the Government officials more readily understood. With some they were better at some times than at other times. In certain periods he got along smoothly with everyone, and at all times he was urgent for improvements."

Despite the unpleasantness with the authorities the journey to Honolulu was a success. The Bishop kept his word and raised a fund for the purchase of building materials and tools, and even the Board of Health, before the pressure of public opinion, arranged for a shipload of lumber.

On the priest's return to Molokai with the welcome news, enthusiasm ran high among the lepers. Everyone who was able turned out to do his or her share towards building the new village. The men, most of whom were minus at least one limb, dragged and carried the lumber into sites that had already been cleared by the women and children. A few of the inmates were found to have a crude knowledge of carpentering. They became men of distinction overnight, and soon the busy music of industrious hammers became a familiar sound. The new cottages were strong and built on solid trestles in order to be able to resist the effects of the storms; they were placed in orderly rows and as each was completed it received its neat coat of clean whitewash.

Miseries were forgotten before the opiate of industry. Men who had been content to await death in a pathetic squalor now gained an interest in life, and in this place where laughter had been forgotten and where each had been for himself community groups now vied with each other in cheerful competition as to who could erect a cottage in the quickest time.

As the village sprang into existence the priest encouraged the planting of gardens. Each little house was given its patch of ground to be cleared and dug for vegetables and flowers, and the same happy improvements and reforms were instituted at the nearby village of Kalaupapa which was also considered a part of the colony. Damien tramped between the villages, exhorting and urging, keeping the flame of enthusiasm at a high pitch. Executive duties alone might have excused him from any physical labor but, unless engaged at a priestly office, he was never to be seen without a hammer, plane or tool of some description in his hand. It was estimated that he actually worked on the building of *three hundred* of the colony's first houses. His own one-room dwelling was erected, with a fearlessness that perhaps was foolhardy, close to the burial ground. It might be wondered why he who was always particular about fresh air and hygienic quarters for his people chose this polluted site for his own house; but there was the practical reason that a great deal of his time was spent in the cemetery. Not only did he have to officiate at the daily burials, his was also the busy office of gravedigger and coffin maker.

CHAPTER VIII

It was about six months after his arrival when he found time to write to his brother and inform him that: "God has deigned to choose your unworthy brother to assist the poor people attacked by that terrible malady, so often mentioned in the Gospel,—leprosy. For the last ten years this plague has been spreading in the islands and at last the Government found itself obliged to isolate those affected with it. Shut up in a corner of the island of Molokai, between inaccessible cliffs and the sea, these unfortunate creatures are condemned to perpetual exile. Out of the *two thousand* in all, who have been sent here, some *eight hundred* are still living, and among them is a certain number of Catholics. A priest was wanted; but here was a difficulty. For, as all communication was forbidden with the rest of the Islands, a priest who should be placed here must consider himself shut up with the lepers for the rest of his life; and Mgr. Maigret, our Vicar-Apostolic, declared that he should not impose this sacrifice on any of us. So, remembering that on the day of my profession I had already put myself under a funeral pall, I offered myself to his Lordship to meet, if he thought it well, this second death. Consequently, on May 11th, a steamer landed me here, together with a batch of fifty lepers, whom the authorities had collected in the Island of Hawaii.

"I found on my arrival a little chapel dedicated to St. Philomena, but that was all. No house to shelter me. I lived a long time under the shelter of a tree, not wishing to sleep under the same roof as the lepers. Later on, the whites of Honolulu having assisted me with their subscriptions, I was able to build myself a hut, sixteen feet long and ten wide, where I am now writing these lines. Well, I have been here six months, surrounded by lepers, and I have not caught the infection: I consider this shows the special protection of our Good God and the Blessed Virgin Mary.

"Leprosy, as far as is known, is incurable; it seems to begin by a corruption of the blood. Discolored patches appear on the skin, especially on the cheeks; and the parts affected lose their feeling. After a time this discoloration covers the entire body; then ulcers begin to open, chiefly at the extremities. The flesh is eaten away, and gives out a fetid odour; even the breath of the leper becomes so foul that the air around is poisoned with it. I have had great difficulty in getting accustomed to such an atmosphere. One day, at a Sunday Mass, I found myself so stifled that I thought I must leave the altar to breathe a little of the outer air, but I restrained myself, thinking of our Lord when he commanded them to open the grave of Lazarus, notwithstanding Mary's words, *jam foetet*. Now my sense of smell does not cause me so much inconvenience. I enter the huts of the lepers without difficulty. Sometimes, indeed, I feel no repugnance when I hear the confessions of those near their end, whose wounds are full of maggots. Often, also, I scarce know how to administer Extreme Unction, when both hands and feet are nothing but raw wounds.

"This may give you some idea of my daily work. Picture to yourself a collection of huts with eight hundred lepers. No doctor; in fact, as there is no cure, there seems no place for a doctor's skill.

"Every morning, then, after my Mass, which is followed by an instruction, I go to visit the sick, half of whom are Catholics. On entering each hut, I begin by offering to hear their confession. Those who refuse this spiritual help, are not, therefore, refused temporal assistance, which is given to all without distinction. Consequently, every one, with the exception of a very few bigoted heretics, look on me as a father. As for me, I make myself a leper, to gain all to Jesus Christ. You may judge by the following fact what a power a missioner has. Last Saturday some of the younger people, discontented with their lot, and thinking themselves ill-treated by the Government, determined on an attempt at revolt. All, except two, were Calvinists or Mormons. Well, I had only to present myself and say a word or two, and all heads were bowed, and all was over!

"I have baptized more than a hundred persons since my arrival. A good part of these died with the white robe of baptismal grace. I have also buried a large number. The average of deaths is at least one a day. Many are so destitute that there is nothing to defray their burial expenses. They are simply wrapped in a blanket. As far as my duties allow me time, I make coffins myself for these poor people. . . ."

The problem of food was not neglected. The original plan of the authorities had been that the lepers should farm and raise their own supplies. After the failure of this ridiculous scheme a small schooner had been sent to the island at irregular intervals with whatever provisions could be bought cheap in Honolulu. A careful selection of proper foods is essential for a leper's well-being. Not the slightest attention was ever shown in this direction and, indeed, even the amounts sent to the colony were always pitifully inadequate. Another hardship often encountered was in the hazardous unloading from the schooners by means of small boats. Bad weather would occasionally cause a capsize and, of course, the loss of provisions. Many a time there was enacted the tragedy of starving lepers standing on the sea-beaten beach and watching with anguished eyes while their only hopes for food were engulfed by the angry waves. These were the conditions existing when the priest came to Molokai.

He rapidly caused a change. Supplies were increased and a steamer with a fixed schedule soon supplanted the haphazard visits of a schooner; but he was never to be completely satisfied with the authorities in this respect and it was to be one of the reasons of his almost ceaseless conflict with them. Even five years after his arrival he was petitioning Honolulu to: "Provide more food!" Ten years later than this appeal he was still begging for the "luxury" of milk.

Other necessities such as clothing, bandages and medicines, were also the subject of his incessant pleas to the authorities. He reported that many of the lepers, with weakened powers of resistance, were dying from the effects of exposure, rather than from their own malady, and that the foulness of their undressed wounds was responsible for the spreading of many other infectious diseases. His first victory along these lines was that the Government sent a few elementary medical supplies and enough materials to establish two small stores, one for each village. Cheap clothing was offered for sale in these establishments and each leper was allowed a generous grant of *six dollars* a year to provide himself with decent apparel. Of course Damien fought to have this pittance increased but he felt some satisfaction because, no matter how small the financial allowance was, it marked a beginning. Along with the gifts, amounting to shiploads, that had been collected by the Bishop and the Sisters it was soon possible for the lepers to abandon their former wretched state of filthy demi-nudity and be clad to a degree that at least insured protection against the elements.

Another of his earlier objects of reform was the "hospital," a tumble-down shed that served as a species of morgue where among scenes of unparalleled horror the friendless dying were deposited to spend their last hours in unheeded misery. Damien rebuilt the building, installed cots, persuaded a few of the more healthy lepers to work as nurses, and, acting as doctor himself, personally washed and bandaged the sores and wounds of each inmate. This latter task he did every morning. It is interesting to note

124

that as late as 1887, just two years before his own end, he was still engaged at the same loathsome task.

All these things he did, and many more, but not for a moment were his spiritual ministrations ever relaxed. Despite the multitudinous claims to his time he managed to build: "another chapel, two miles from this, at the other end of our settlement." * Of course he once again occupied his usual roles of builder, carpenter and laborer. Mentioning this, he tells his parents:

"I am not ashamed to act as mason or carpenter, when it is for the glory of God. These ten years I have been on the mission I have built a church or chapel every year. The habit I had at home of practising different kinds of work, is of immense use to me here."

Church services became a popular event in the settlement and were attended, in increasing numbers, not only by Catholics but by Protestants and non-Christians who were attracted by the pageantry and the music. Apart from religious significance the ceremonies of his Church were the only entertainment the lepers had, and perhaps recognizing this fact Damien was careful to observe the niceties of ritual. Mass was always celebrated with the utmost pomp and the congregations became so crowded that the priest was able to report to the Bishop that:

"I hope I shall please your Lordship by acquainting you that, since the time I left you to come here, a great change has been brought about in the general spirit of the population. Already, for three Sundays consecutively I had hardly room enough for my parishioners, Christians and Catechumens. Yesterday, I was obliged to place those of my Christians who attend Mass regularly during the week outside the chapel, the men on one side and the women on the other along the windows. Not less than thirty persons were left outside, and the inside of the chapel was so

* Kalaupapa.

filled that one could scarcely have passed. I baptize the neophytes by dozens and half-dozens every week. Besides the attendance at Mass, we hold gatherings on Sunday evenings for the infirm. At Kalawao, alone, four and sometimes five homes are filled *a ku mawaho*—to running over; these reunions are presided over by my *luna*—prayer-leaders. As to myself, after the Mass and baptisms, I take some breakfast and then start at once on my way to Kalaupapa, where I have three different gatherings: one for the old Christians of the district who are not lepers, another for the sick residing near the landing place, and a third for those who live in the prominent part of the Settlement; these last are thirty in number. I have not yet had time to leave the Settlement. The weekly visit of all my sick parishioners takes most of my time. Next week, however, I hope once more to visit the whole island if my foot, which is a little swollen from a wound, is healed.

"I do not know what it is that requires my most urgent attention. The Chapel at Kaluaha is absolutely necessary, but I shall not have time to do it myself, for it would keep me too long away from my dying parishioners at Kalawao. The church of St. Philomena (here) must at all costs be enlarged ten feet at least. The most urgent demands are made for it. . . . However, '*He mea lealea no u wa hana kamana*'—the work of carpenter is pleasant to me."

Indeed, it was his only hobby; the rare moments that he had to himself were spent making window frames, doors and various small objects of furniture which would be distributed as gifts to all who would use them.

He was the only priest on Molokai and there were non-leper Catholics dwelling beyond the tall cliffs that walled the settlement. They were not to remain unvisited for long. Paying no attention to the ban of the authorities he strapped a portable altar to his back, scaled the mountains, and made a tour of the entire island. He found that there were enough Catholics to justify an establishment of a new parish and he wrote the Bishop suggesting that if a new missionary were sent to administer to the non-lepers he (Damien) would be free to devote his entire time to where he was so urgently needed; and that, also, there then would be no cause for him further to antagonize the Board of Health by breaking the law of isolation. Msgr. Maigret, who always cooperated when it was in his power, responded to the plea by sending Father Andrew Burgermann.

When this priest arrived Damien let him remain in the settlement whilst he himself once again climbed the mountains, staying on the southern side of the island until he had built a new church. This building was quite pretentious for the island, being forty-four feet long and twenty-two feet wide and even possessing a tower fifty feet high. While slaving away at this work the priest lodged, in turn, at the dwellings of his parishioners. Because of these circumstances there occurred an incident which was of sufficient importance for him to relate several years later to Brother Dutton, who writes of it as follows: "He told me that one night when in one of these huts a young native woman being about to sleep near him, he left the house and stayed outdoors. . . ." A sparsely worded story but fifteen years after it happened it still remains a disturbing memory to Damien. One wonders what his thoughts were, waking in that dim interior and startled by the proximity of the young woman. Perhaps she had no motive in choosing her couch so close to his, but this supposition is extremely doubtful when one reflects how loose a code of morals was practised by a majority of the natives at that time. And he was everything that would appeal to such a woman; he was a person of distinction and was blessed with a strong and magnificent physique. If she had been a wanton he had vows that were a challenge to her charms and willingness. The circumstances and environment probably would have served to create a strong temptation for most men, and it must be remembered that Damien was only thirty-four years old and in full possession of a splendid

manhood, but. . . . "he left the house and stayed outdoors."

In this same statement Dutton adds,

"The question of his purity has been brought up in the
public prints. I merely state my firm belief that he was
wholly devoid of sensuality during the time I knew him.
. . . It never occurred to me to question his lifelong ad-
herence to virtue. He seemed, while I knew him at least, to
have no thoughts of such things. The charges (by the Rev.
Mr. Hyde) since his death are not new ones; I heard some
while he was living. That is, the parties so informing me
said that Father Damien was innocent of the charges except in so far as he apparently unwittingly gave grounds
for suspicion by his want of caution in allowing women to
be about his house, being apparently blind to what might
seem evil in the eyes of others."

On completing the building of the new chapel Damien
returned to the leper settlement and delivered the keys to
Father Andrew, interrupting that priest's speech of gratitude by declaring that the short sojourn away from Kalawao had been a "vacation" for him and that "the manual
labor and the pure air outside the settlement were exceedingly good for my health!"

They said their farewells and Damien resumed his routine. A species of rough surgery, based on a knowledge
gleaned from a medical book, was now added to his other
accomplishments and many a rotting bone or dead limb
was removed by him. He had no operating chamber, glittering with magnificent apparatus, nor did he even have, as
he delved into putrid flesh, the comforting protection of
rubber gloves. His sole prophylactics were soap and water
and he worked on a bare plank table with a few odd tools
as his only instruments. Anaesthesia was not needed, it being one of the characteristics of leprosy that the most
afflicted portions of the body are decayed to a point beyond any feeling. Disagreeable though this task must have

been, it still was not as distressful or as dangerous in the medical sense as his daily duty of listening to confessions. Leprosy greatly affects the larynx and with many lepers the voice gradually decreases until it is but a faint whisper. In such cases the priest, while listening to the penitent, had to lean so close that the foul breath struck him full in the face. There were other occasions even worse. Sometimes the leper develops a kind of asthma which brings on sudden coughs attended by hemorrhages of black blood and several times this horrible expectoration was unavoidably ejected over the priest. So common were these occurrences that he made it a habit when listening to confessions to have at hand a basin and towel.

CHAPTER IX

Yet, despite the hardships and personal discomfort it involved on himself, he was always encouraging and stressing the importance of the confessional act as a means to bring spiritual comfort. There are many accusations brought by non-Catholics against this institution and the statement is often heard that they cannot understand how one man can kneel before another and tell what may be the innermost secrets of his mind and body. But when a Catholic kneels before the confessor and utters the words, "Pray, Father, bless me, for I have sinned" and the response comes back to him, "The Lord be in thy heart and on thy lips, that thou mayest truly and humbly confess thy sins, in the name of the Father, and of the Son, and of the Holy Ghost" the relationship is no longer merely between two fellowmen. The penitent, by his faith, is a participant in an essential part of the Sacrament of Penance as prescribed by Jesus Christ; and the confessor, because of that same faith, is a successor of the Apostles, divinely commissioned and trained by years of study and prayer with the right and duty to pass judgment on men's sins. What he hears is in absolute secret bound by the seal of the confessional and never to be divulged, not even if his own or any other life were at stake. No one can deny that since the beginning of Christianity there have been rascals who have worn the priestly habit, but it is a striking fact that down through those long centuries there have been but few instances of the seal of the confessional being violated.

Because of this secrecy an air of mystery, sometimes sinister, sometimes glamorous, has grown to envelop the confessor and his duties. Actually, and apart from the sacramental aspect, it must be an irksome task for the priesthood. Neither glamorous nor mysterious can it be for them to sit hours at a time in a stuffy box-like compartment, week after week, year after year, listening to the same —for even in his errors man is seldom startlingly different— repetitious story of weaknesses, hopes and vanities. It is a human trait to seek comfort by telling one's troubles to someone else and today, by sympathetically fostering that characteristic, specialists in psychiatry are enabled to make exceedingly lucrative livings; but no doctor, no matter how famous his name or how high sounding his degrees or how worthy his services, can give the contentment that the gift of absolution brings a sincere penitent in the confessional. To such a penitent descends a supreme peace that eases the conscience and obliterates the perplexities of past misdoings.

Such solace, the assurance of divine pardon, was necessary in the life of the staunch Catholic whose unwavering faith had brought him to dreary Molokai. He was not the kind of missionary who, because he taught the consciousness of sin, imagined he was personally exempt from that inevitable mark of man. He labored under no false delusions regarding his faults; his being a priest served only to make his standards more exacting and his self-examinations more rigorous as to how he kept those standards.

The seriousness with which he regarded the obligations of the confessional is shown on the occasion when the Provincial of his Order tried to visit him during the time when the law of isolation was being enforced. Damien had not seen anybody from the outside world for several months and on the calm morning when the little steamer blew a blast from its whistle and hove to off Kalawao it must have presented a welcome sight to his eyes. He rushed to launch a boat and, with several of the more fit lepers rowing, put off to the steamer where, at that very moment, the captain was refusing the request of the Provincial that he be allowed to go ashore for even half an hour.

As Damien's boat came alongside the vessel and as his hand sought the accommodation ladder the captain warned him not to come aboard, reminding him of the new law. The disappointed priest pleaded that all he wished was a few minutes alone and in privacy with his Superior so that he could make his confession. The captain retorted that he had no alternative but to obey the command of the authorities.

"Then," said Damien, "I shall make my confession here."

The hubbub of the ship's life died down and a stillness enveloped the decks as he knelt in the sternsheets of his tiny craft which was rising and falling with the slow motion of the easy swell. The Provincial took his place at the rail above, and this courageous act of self-abasement that was so thorough and complete began before the casual eyes of the ship's passengers and crew who thronged the upper deck in interested groups, staring down, some awed, some puzzled, but all silent.

The final words of contrition came, the sentence of penance, the murmured balm of absolution, then the priest, taking his seat once again, made a gesture to his crew. The oars dipped and the boat gathered way on the calm water, slipping quickly from the shadow of the steamer's bulk. Except for a deliberate upraising of an arm in silent salute to his Superior, Damien ignored the ship. With his gaze fixed on the shore, he sat, steering the boat, a rigid figure with both hands gripping the tiller bar. Never once did he look behind and the audience who had witnessed the baring of his soul were as disregarded as though they had never existed. They stared after him until the creak of rowlocks could no longer be heard, until the flash of the oar blades was lost in the foam of the surf. They watched him and his lepers scramble on the rocky beach, dragging the boat after them.

Even after the ship sailed a heavy, uneasy silence persisted along the steamer's decks. The motley throng of mixed races and of varying or of no creeds that made up the ship's company, these men who lived adventurous lives in remote places and who saluted personal courage as being the first of human graces, had been stilled to an unusual quietude, profound and respectful before a kind of bravery that was new to them. And to their credit it must be said that when the steamer arrived in Honolulu and they were met by journalists, not one word of what they heard on that peaceful morning was repeated. However, news of the incident reached the ears of the French Consul, representative of the nation that had first sponsored and protected the activities of the Catholic missionaries in Hawaii. That official immediately lodged a vigorous complaint with the authorities. The result was that, with the active help of another Frenchman who was serving on the Board of Health, the law of isolation was modified to a more sensible and less stringent degree.

Not least among Damien's reforms at Molokai was his success in removing the fear of death from the minds of his parishioners.

"From morning till night (he tells Pamphile) I am in the midst of physical and moral miseries which rend my heart. Nevertheless I endeavor to show myself always cheerful, that I may raise the courage of the weak. I place death before their eyes as the end of all their evil. . . . Many in consequence look upon death with a resignation and sometimes with joy."

The paralyzing effects of despair and hopelessness that had been so characteristic of the settlement were dissolved before his continual persuasions that the hardships of disease were but passing incidents on the threshold of a new

133

and eternal life; a life that the Divine compassion made it possible for all to enter. With the magic of hope even the daily funeral ceremonies took on somewhat of a festive air, although religious solemnity was never neglected. He founded "two different associations; both have for an object the carrying out of burials in a becoming manner." The idea of the plurality was that, with his usual shrewdness, he saw that if there were only one such organization enthusiasm might flag, but with two the spirit of competition would always hold the interest.

In Honolulu the Bishop had collected drums, flutes, guitars and even a few brass horns; the Sisters sent ribbons and gaily colored cloths; and at the settlement it soon became a great privilege to be allowed to join the padre's burial associations. Feminine members wore red and white sashes and the men usually played or carried some instrument in the band.

The Hawaiians are noted for their love of music in all its forms. Damien was quick to utilize this trait in his war against the spirit of pessimism. He formed choirs that were in reality entire community groups of singers, and almost every evening a crowd of men, women, and children, would gather under the trees near the church. Their language, so soft and harmonious, is admirably suited for chanting, and to the European ear the plaintive quality that marks almost all their songs has a note of sadness that is not unpleasant. Sometimes new airs and hymns were improvised to fit their tragic environment and one in particular was the favorite of the young women. To an outsider the words seem indescribably sorrowful but their soft voices could be heard singing it on every occasion. Translated, it reads:

> When, oh when shall it be given to me
> To behold my God?
> When,
> Oh, when shall the captivity of my wretched soul

Cease in this strange land where night and day
Weeping,
Weeping alone is my portion;
When, oh when shall I leave this valley of sorrow,
Where the only bread I eat is my continual tears?
When, oh when shall I see my well-beloved Lord?
Prince of the Heavens is He,
Guardian of my soul, my Hope, my Saviour,
My All. . . .

The priest strove hard to dispel the gloomy note that is unfortunately usually associated with religion. The exterior of the church at Kalawao was painted, much to the amusement of visitors, in a variety of bright colors, for he knew the susceptibility of the Hawaiian to gaudiness. Never was there an occasion missed that might serve as an opportunity for a celebration of some sort; consequently there were numerous religious processions and festivals, followed by picnics.

That of the Corpus Christi was a particularly gay affair, attended by everybody in the colony who could walk. As it was one of the great events of the year both villages would be busy with preparations for weeks in advance. Flowers would be collected and woven into fragrant wreaths, special clothes would be fashioned for the acolytes, and sashes and rosettes made for all. The actual day would be noisy with drums and bright with flags, there would be singing under the direction of a

"blind leper (writes Damien, describing such an occasion) who is very clever at directing music, and who does it with perfect precision and sureness. To see it would be sufficient to rouse jealousy in your best cathedral choirs. . . . The cross heads the procession and is followed by a magnificent banner; the brass instruments with drums come next. Two Hawaiian flags wave over the two rival associations of natives. Long files of women are seen next; then the men also marching in rows, followed next by my choir of

135

forty voices, always under the direction of my good blind *Petero*. A healthy man walks by his side to protect him with a sunshade from the burning rays of the sun. The thurifers and the children who strewed flowers formed the immediate vanguard of the King of Kings; four rough torches adorned with verdure and flowers formed the escort around the canopy, and a portable altar gracefully adorned, helped to add to the beauty of the retinue. . . . After the ceremony, a good and hearty meal, which had been prepared the day before, was served to all. . . . You see, therefore, that our Lord permits us now and then to pick a beautiful rose among sharp thorns."

Strange pageantry it must have been in that tropic setting. To a visitor the music and fluttering of banners, among those pitiably disfigured and crippled people, might probably have seemed tragically incongruous; but to the lepers, already marked by death, such symbols of happiness served not only to inspire hope of the future life, but to give them a blessed forgetfulness of their present miseries.

By such means and by every ingenuity he could devise Damien sought to obliterate the depressing stigma that the name of the disease had accumulated through the centuries. In every way he tried to make his people forget that they had ever been considered "unclean" or outcasts. His work was not confined to those of his own religion, for although he had come to Molokai as a Catholic priest he remained to serve all.

Under the circumstances it is not surprising that there were many conversions but, as at his earlier parishes, he made sure that the applicants, except in cases of dire emergency, were suitably instructed before receiving them into the Church. All aspirants were solemnly warned that, after baptism, they would be expected to attend regularly to their Catholic duties. He knew every one of his parishioners by name and history and he knew well who were fit enough to attend Mass. On Sundays the congregations would be

136

counted; if any members of his flock were missing he would be at their huts quickly enough, sternly inquiring as to the reason for the absence. Discipline sometimes tempered his kindness although he found that:

"I must almost in every house change my methods. At one time I speak words of sweetness and consolation; at another I must add some bitterness because there is a sinner who refuses to open his eyes; and even as the thunder sometimes rolls with vehemence, so I now and again threaten a hardened soul with terrible chastisements, and this has often had good effects."

At the commencement of his third year at the settlement he was notified that the Bishop, after receiving the necessary permission, intended to pay him an official visit of several days' duration. Here, indeed, was a splendid opportunity for festivity. The news was announced in both chapels and there followed a week of happy preparation. It was the first time such an important dignitary had signified an intention of staying at the colony and the lepers intended to show their gratitude by making his visit the most gala, for them, of occasions.

The great morning arrived (June 8, 1875) when the steamer anchored off the shore. Every inmate of the settlement who could walk was on the rocky beach to greet the venerable Bishop. The band played, flags waved, and as Monseigneur Maigret affectionately greeted Damien a cheer was offered with voices that were, as Father Albert Montitor, who was accompanying the Bishop recorded, "hoarse from the disease."

All that day the settlement was inspected. As each improvement was noted by his Superior, Damien sought to point out how much further need there was for progress and help. His own work he belittled and grew quite confused when, in a speech that came as a complete surprise to him, one of the older natives addressed the Bishop, thanking him for allowing Damien to live in their midst.

"He overwhelms us," said the man in his own language, "with his solicitous care, and he himself builds our houses. When any one of us is ill, he gives him tea, biscuits and sugar; and to the poor he gives clothes. He makes no distinction between Catholics and Protestants."

In the evening Damien served his guests hot breadfruit and fresh pork, baked after the native fashion. After the meal had been finished a large number of the parishioners came to serenade with the band. Whatever picturesque aspect this usually romantic proceeding might have had for the thoroughly observant Father Montitor was thoroughly spoiled when, in the luminous light of a full moon, he was horrified to see:

"The musicians had for the most part only two or three fingers, and their lips were very much swollen with leprosy; yet they played, with great success, many different pieces, and entertained us for two whole hours."

Included among the many gifts brought by the charitable Bishop were surplices and robes for the altar boys and these were displayed for the first time on the following Sunday when pontifical High Mass was celebrated. The youthful acolytes, faces already distorted with the disease, seemed to forget their pitiful distress in the enormous pride they felt at being seen in the white and scarlet splendors of the new garb and they performed their duties well before the gaze of the aged Prelate who sat in his chair, watching every detail of the ritual with a sad and grave interest.

It was a splendid exhibition of faith. Not only the chapel but the surrounding grounds were crowded with worshipers, on nearly all of whom there was fixed the seal of approaching death. Scarcely a member of the packed congregation was there whose face or body did not carry the loathsome marks of the disease. The Bishop wept openly when the voices of the choir rose in a creditable, despite the hoarseness of the tainted throats, rendition of one of

Mozart's Masses. The distant boom, sad and persistent, of the surf was a fit accompaniment to the solemn ceremony and the murmur of the clean sea wind, rustling the nearby foliage, must have been a provocative sound to poor Father Montitor who experienced a considerable difficulty in fighting a mounting sense of nausea. To him, on that hot morning, the crowded chapel was "a chamber of horrors; the very air being polluted with the fetid odor of a charnel-house."

That same day one hundred and thirty-five of the newly-baptized, both adults and children, knelt before the Bishop to be confirmed. The chapel was bright with flowers and candles and among the people there was a brave display of ribbons and rosettes and sashes. It was an important and happy occasion marred only by the disagreeable fact that on some foreheads scarcely a sound spot could be found to receive the holy anointing.

The episcopal stay lasted five days in all. On the last evening the priest and his guests sat in the dusk and talked of Europe. Anecdotes were related of homes and family. They spoke in French. Although for the most part Damien was content to remain a listener, he argued with Montitor for a few minutes over the merits of the River Laak as a skating ground until the Bishop jocularly reminded them of their surroundings and the almost certainty of their never seeing ice again. Pipes were puffed in silence for a while and then the conversation turned to languages. Damien remarked that through long non-usage he found he had no longer a ready command of Flemish and that the composing of his letters to his mother, who was now getting on in years, was becoming increasingly difficult.

"What age is she?" asked the Bishop.

"She was born in 1804," said Damien.

"So then," replied the other, "your mother is the same age as myself. Give her my greetings."

Farewells were said the next morning. Before he stepped into the steamer's boat the Bishop blessed the crowd which respectfully knelt for a last benediction; then as a parting gift, he distributed a handful of holy medals to the children who had come to wave goodbye. Those children, most of them orphans, had been the subject of a long conversation between him and Damien, for without any natural protectors to give them the care and attention their plight so urgently demanded they were becoming one of the colony's most distressing problems. One of Damien's first actions after arriving had been to persuade the adults to give some degree of shelter to the homeless youngsters. His work in this direction had been forced to cease before the more important tasks involving the general needs of the colony.

Now, however, with a little money that the Bishop had left for this purpose, he was able to set about building a house that was to serve as an orphanage. When it was completed he installed an elderly woman, widow of a leper, to act as a combination cook, housekeeper and matron. Of a necessity this institution was very small at the commencement and only a few inmates could be accepted. These were selected from the most pitiable cases among the girl children and for them the Government agent was persuaded to issue an official weekly ration of meat and *taro*. To supplement this meager and sometimes irregular fare the priest planted a large field of sweet potatoes; then, too, he could always depend on the steady help of the Sisters in Honolulu who, by dint of successful appeals to kindhearted citizens, were enabled to keep up a continual flow of gifts to Molokai. Indeed, as a result of their efforts he was soon able to build a similar home for the boys. Later, both institutions were repeatedly increased in size until they eventually were to be splendidly staffed with nurses and schoolmasters.

But this progress took many years and in the early days the priest was grateful enough when he was able to provide a roof and food for his sick waifs. As for the offices of instructor and nurse, he was both. It was to be a long wait before even a resident doctor came to lighten his burden. Until that time arrived, native *kokuas* (helpers) whom he personally had trained were to be his sole assistants.

CHAPTER X

The days went by. If their passage was slow and made tedious with the uninterrupted repetition of his work, or if because of that same reason they sped by, *velis et remis*, with merciful haste, no one was ever to know. It seems that surely there were times when even he must have paused, overwhelmed with the apparent hopelessness of his position. Like a swimmer fallen from a ship in a stormy sea he was alone; fresh difficulties, like angry waves, relentless and unceasing, advanced to meet him all sides. He had a tremendous and unwavering faith, tenacity of purpose and rugged physical strength. Nevertheless he was but one man, and sometimes his efforts must have seemed pitifully futile in the gigantic morass of trouble and despair that was Molokai.

Not one of the reforms established by him was accomplished with ease, and having been established not one would have survived a week without his aggressive support. He brought order to this lawless and abandoned community, but to his death there remained desperate characters who sought, by every conceivable means, to outwit him or his work. And to the end there remained a steady flow of new perplexities and disappointments to harass him.

He lived, of course, with the utmost simplicity. Two meals a day were his limit; a late morning meal, usually consisting of rice, meat, coffee and a few "hard tack" biscuits; and in the evening he would "take what was left at dinner, with a cup of tea, the water for which I boil over a lamp. I only take two meals a day. It is rarely I taste anything between. You see I live very well; I do not starve and I am not much at home in the daytime."

After darkness he would light the lamp and read his breviary; then, perhaps, he would spend a half hour or so at his useful hobby of carpentering, or he might write to, or re-read one of the precious letters from, Tremeloo. Or he might stroll for a while in the adjoining graveyard. To Pamphile he tells something of the peace he felt at these times: "The cemetery, church and my house form one enclosure; thus at night time I am the sole keeper of this garden of the dead, where my spiritual children lie at rest." And sometimes, weary after a hard day spent in the foul interior of the "hospital" he would stroll amongst the graves of his cemetery, saying his beads and meditating "on that unending happiness which so many of them (the dead) are enjoying. I confess to you, my dear brother, the cemetery and the hut of the dying are my best meditation books."

Such philosophy must have been of value to him when the news came that his father had died. Death to him who saw much of it was never to hold any terrors. Life on this earth, as he taught and preached to the suffering lepers, was merely a temporary phase, a fleeting moment in the vastness of eternity. After his first moments of sadness at his parent's death he wrote to Tremeloo words of sympathy that ended with: "the loss we have sustained must have been a sore grief to you. But what would you? Almighty God intends to teach you not to attach yourselves to the things of this world. Let us remember that it is a place of exile, and that those who die in the Lord are far happier than you or I who are left here below."

Letters from his family were, except for an occasional religious paper, his only link with Europe. For the most part they were stilted epistles, confined to news of relatives or a polite and brief mention of village events. Frontiers were changing that decade. France, for a third time, had decided to be a Republic and the Queen of England had

143

been proclaimed Empress of India, but of these events the missionary on the far-off island seems never to have heard. Nor was he ever to show much interest in the outside world; even when it offered him its homage he remained indifferent. The demands of his own little world, whose boundaries began with the rocky precipices a few miles behind, were enough to keep him occupied. To him the plight of his lepers was infinitely more tragic than the distant drama of history.

Yet, at this time (the same year he received his Bishop) there was printed in the Norwegian newspapers a story that would undoubtedly have caught his interest if he had seen it. At Bergen, the scientist Armauer Hansen, was able, after several years of difficult labor, to demonstrate that he had discovered and could isolate the bacteria of leprosy. Perhaps it was just as well Damien was never to know of this great work because it might have given him a hope for his lepers that could never have been realized. Hansen had won a memorable battle in the conflict against the disease but it was not a complete victory. Nor has that victory been achieved to the present day. The bacillus has been isolated, but beyond and before this fact, there still remains the same mystery that baffled the ancient Egyptians.

Since Hansen's discovery countless experiments have been made with the dread microbe. Strangely enough it does not seem to be communicable when the ordinary methods of injection are used. Hansen inoculated rabbits, cats and monkeys, but they stayed healthy. Köbner with the same result experimented for years on fish, frogs and guinea-pigs. Professors Marchoux and Stanziale conducted exhaustive trials, injecting the germs in the most sensitive portion of an animal's anatomy, the eye. Brave men, such as Dr. Danielssen, have even permitted the matter from a leper's wound to be injected into their own blood streams, but beyond the appearance of a few septic sores there has been no result. Although leprosy is certainly contagious, science is still at a loss to know the means of its communicability.

Although a definite and complete cure has not yet been found and although little is still known about the disease, there has been some progress made in the treatment. In 1915 Sir Leonard Rogers was able to announce a formula and treatment which, in many cases, has had brilliant results. The treatment used today at Molokai, based on injections of derivatives of chaulmoogra oil, is the result of work of a young Negro chemist, Miss Alice Ball, of the University of Hawaii, whose health gave way before the long hours she spent in research. After she died the experiments were completed by her colleagues and the findings are giving relief to many a leper today; but there remains to be discovered a specific prescription that will definitely counteract the *bacillus leprae*. Research workers of all nations continue to labor valiantly; Dr. Ernest Muir, now of London and late of Calcutta, who has diligently studied the disease for over thirty years; Dr. Heiser, late of Manila and the U. S. Public Health Service; Dr. Ryrie of Malaya; C. D. Leake of California, and many others. "Discoveries" are being constantly reported by an over-enthusiastic press, but the fact remains that a cure has not yet been found.

The years marched on. Damien was yet in his thirties, still young according to the world's reckoning, but regarded as a patriarch by the outcasts of Molokai. He looked the part. In appearance he seemed at least ten years more than his actual age. Toil had thickened his figure from slimness to a broad sturdiness. Hardships and rigorous self-discipline had exacted an inevitable toll on his face. Gray was beginning to temper his hair. His eyes, already weakened through excessive reading during student days, were suffering from the continual glare of the tropic sun. And his sober mannerisms were those of a much older man; the gravity of spirit and seriousness of mind that were so characteristic of him during adolescence had become more emphasized in the gloomy environment of the settlement.

But if laughter was rare to him it did not mean that he was of the lugubrious type who on the basis of their own somber righteousness seek to prevent the pleasures of others. He encouraged rather than frowned upon a pleasing custom that had come into being whereby a score or so of his parishioners would come and visit him every day whilst he had his evening meal. Squatting in a circle around him, for he ate outdoors, they would regale each other and him with noisy stories and anecdotes. Good-humored arguments might take place, a guitar perhaps would tinkle and always, sooner or later, songs would be chanted. The hour was in the late afternoon, just before dusk when the long shadows cooled the island and the oblique rays of the sinking sun, with a final brightness, made the tree-tops dance in a golden shimmer. These gatherings grew to be such popular functions that they acquired, in the native language, the definite and poetic name of "Time-of-peace-between-night-and-day," and as the light faded and Damien sipped his tea before the friendly eyes of his audience, he would, sometimes, be forced to answer innumerable questions about his own country and village, but more often he would be allowed to remain silent while the others talked. The Hawaiians like to talk and the lepers were no exception to this racial trait. With a folk-lore that is exceedingly rich to draw upon there was never any scarcity of legends. Damien, who enjoyed the ancient tales, spent many a pleasant hour listening to the exploits of the early Hawaiian heroes.

After he had finished eating Damien would brew over a small lamp a kettle of tea. As six battered cups were all he possessed it would become a matter of boisterous competition among his guests to decide who was to drink with him. His pipe would be lit and everybody was free to borrow it for a few puffs. He showed the same hospitality to all and in everything. The door of his hut was never locked and as he was absent most of the day he let it be known that anybody who so wished could enter and rest on his bed. By this time he seems to have been absolutely without fear as far as the disease was concerned. Having won the lepers' confidence he adhered to his policy of never showing repulsion or disgust at their ailment. His persistent lack of precaution has been criticized, but he probably realized that he could not escape permanently, however careful he might be. Or perhaps he remembered and sought to emulate the example set by Ignatius Loyala and his followers, Francis Xavier and Simon Rodriguez, all of whom had shared their beds and food with the most loathsome of lepers.

CHAPTER XI

As the nineteenth century matured the Kingdom of Hawaii was becoming a factor of great importance in the diplomatic sportings between the larger nations. Development of Pacific trade had brought Honolulu the happy name of "Crossroads of the Pacific," but commercial prosperity was not the only reason why statesmen and admirals were conferring in distant chancelleries. The increasing value of the islands as a naval base was a fact too obvious to escape the attention of strategists whose distances were shortening and whose problems were multiplying with the installation of steam in their fleets.

Foreign naval captains no longer trained their guns on Honolulu town with haughty demands to barefooted chieftains. Subtler methods were now used by the great powers. Legations had been established and gold-braided ministers bringing fraternal messages from the heads of their countries, bowed low and their ladies curtsied at the court of the island kingdom. Of course, intrigue flourished but it was against an agreeable pageantry of royal festivity and stately dinners. The etiquette of Windsor became the ritual of the tropical palace and was observed with the utmost decorum both by the European diplomatists and by native subjects. Under the hot sun the suave Europeans might sweat in their cocked hats, but the gleam of their uniform was a pleasant if ominous flattery to the dusky monarchs before whom they bent their knee and to whom they brought princely gifts of magnificent plate and jeweled symbols of ancient orders of chivalry which had supplanted the bright calicos and gaudy bead offerings of a few decades earlier. Actually a group of American traders and planters had gained control of the government by this time. In fact those gentry, who in many cases were the descendants of the Protestant missionaries, occupied most of the cabinet and official positions, but to the end of the monarchy the kingly office, because of the sincere veneration borne toward it by the majority of the native population, remained sufficiently important to merit and receive royal prerogatives.

When in 1881 the then ruling monarch, Kalahaua, accompanied by his Chamberlain and Commissioner of Immigration (both Americans) and a suitable retinue, set out on a tour of the world he was received with splendid hospitality in every land he visited. Batteries roared the royal salute and soldiers paraded in his honor in the United States, in Japan and in China. The famous Li Hung Chang, happy at the prospect of a new truce with Russia, tendered him a magnificent banquet. In Siam a colorful ruler showed him the full glories of his Kingdom. The royal entertainment continued under the auspices of the Sultan of Johore and in India innumerable potentates vied with each other in fantastic exhibitions of lavish hospitality. Europe was not neglected in the triumphant tour and each capital, to the thudding of inevitable guns, paid the King of Hawaii the correct homage due to his rank.

The Queen, Kapiolani, remained in Honolulu. As she was a simple and retiring person, content and indeed anxious to remain in the privacy of the palace, the royal duties were assumed by the King's sister, the Princess Liliuokalani, who as Heir Apparent to the throne, had been proclaimed Regent during His Majesty's absence. This position proved to be no sinecure as far as she was concerned. While her absent brother was engaged in his fraternal frolickings with other exalted dynasts, she was responsible for many improvements in the Government administration.

It was only natural that the attention of such a woman should be turned to notorious Molokai. Damien's name was not unknown in Honolulu and reports of his courage were even beginning, much to his dismay, to spread to more distant countries. He deplored any form of publicity and when his brother allowed one of his letters to be printed in a Catholic missionary journal he wrote to him with some asperity: "Once for all let me tell you that I do not like that done. I want to be unknown to the world, and now I find, in consequence of the few letters I have written, that I am being talked about on all sides, even in America."

Not all the talk was admiration. He was still a thorn in the side of the Board of Health at Honolulu. In certain circles he was still heartily disliked as an aggressive nuisance whose continual pleas for better conditions could not be quieted. In vain the officials tried to answer his demands with explanations involving "budgets" and "limitations of fiscal allotments." With exasperation they reminded him that the settlement had improved immeasurably during the last few years. A government superintendent had been installed; no longer were the lepers in danger of starvation; and, as a final luxury, a resident doctor had been promised. But still the priest kept at his incessant pleas; the unreasonable fellow wanted better food, more clothing, even *attendants* for the expected doctor.

When the Regent made known her intention of visiting Molokai the officials were profoundly surprised, even shocked. But she was not to be dissuaded. Two weeks after her decision, flanked by a numerous party, she embarked aboard the steamer "Lehua," and although certain of the authorities might mutter at this voyage on the part of Her Royal Highness, it proved to be highly popular with the rest of her subjects who showed their opinion by making the departure of the royal party a gala event. Crowds lined the entire harbor front, waving farewells, and shouting approval at the Princess Regent's thoughtful and courageous act.

Damien had worked feverishly in making preparations

for his distinguished guest. When the "Lehua," presenting a brave sight with new paint glimmering in the morning sunlight and with the large crimson and gold royal standard fluttering splendidly from her maintruck, dropped anchor off Kalaupapa landing, her passengers could see a crowd of some eight hundred lepers, all of the colony able to walk, drawn up on the beach to receive them. The sashes and banners of the burial associations had been utilized for the occasion, and of course the band was in great evidence. Near the landing stood a triumphal arch festooned with wild flowers; around it the priest had mustered the less terrifying of his charges into two ranks, to form a guard of honor. The children were placed to scatter flowers along the pathway of the Royal procession.

Great and happy and sincere was the commotion as the Princess was rowed ashore. Cheers were given and her name shouted with wild enthusiasm as the band blared the National Anthem. The ovation continued as she set foot on the beach and after having greeted Damien was escorted by him through the garlanded arch, past the guard of honor, to a dais that had been especially erected for this moment.

Onto the platform she stepped, a tall woman with a majestic appearance suited to her birth, wearing a black dress unadorned save for a sprinkling of flowers around the neck. Visibly moved by the welcome she held up a hand and the cheers gradually died away to an expectant silence. She gazed upon the sea of disease-ravaged yet cheerful faces that were so eagerly turned to her and so obviously waiting for the words that never came, for try as she could, the Princess was not able to find voice. Her lips trembled and tears flooded her eyes, and turning to one of her staff, she made a gesture for him to speak in her stead.

The schedule of the visit only called for one hour ashore but she insisted on remaining the entire day, with the priest showing her almost every part of the settlement, but beyond his simple explanations and her questions there was not much conversation between them. The peasant-born priest from Belgium and the daughter of Polynesian Chieftains seemed to understand each other well without many words.

The horror of seeing those unfortunate beings who were in the advanced stages of the disease was spared her as much as possible although once, while passing the open doors of the "hospital," she saw something that forced her to turn away and seek the arm of a lady-in-waiting for support, shutting her eyes as though trying to erase what she had just seen. And it was then she told Damien it was hard to believe that anyone should stay in this tragic place of his own free will.

Her words were a tribute but he seemed puzzled.

"It is my work," he explained with simplicity. "You see, Madame, they are my parishioners."

Before replying her eyes roved from him to the pitiful crowd that followed close behind.

"Your parishioners," she said softly, "and my people."

It was night before the anxious captain of the "Lehua" was informed that his royal passenger was ready to return. And it was a fine night. High above the tall dark outline of the island precipices rolled a majestic bank of clouds from behind which spilled the glow of a full moon, a veil of stars curtained the rest of the sky, the sea was flat and on the beach the dancing flames and shifting shadows of festive bonfires made the beauty complete.

The leave-taking of the Princess was inexpressibly sad. The lepers chanted *oliolis*, melancholy recitatives that, like the sagas sung by the bards of ancient Ireland, told of the glories and victories of the ancestors of the royal house of Hawaii. Sometimes all would sing in chorus, sometimes the women would wail alone or it might be that the men would carry the refrain for a few minutes; the chanting never ceased until the steamer had sailed. Nor was music the only ceremony. Flanking the Princess as she walked to the landing were men carrying lighted *kukui*-nuts bound in ti-leaves, torches that blazed and flared and gave off eddying clouds of white smoke. The burning of those nuts was one of the zealously guarded symbols of the ancient royalty and was a distinction granted only to personal retainers. Solemnly and showing their pride at being allowed this privilege the leprous torchbearers stood as erect as their disease allowed them, grouped in a half-circle, a sad parody of a military formation, while their Princess said farewell to the priest.

The moment was not without its note of gallantry. As she stepped into the waiting boat she extended her hand to Damien who, with a sudden impulse, bent low and kissed it.

The oars dipped and the boat surged forward, and every time each oar touched the water a shower of phosphorescent sparks was kindled. The chanting rose in volume and Liliuokalani, silhouetted against the sky and sea, standing in the sternsheets of the little boat, waved goodbye to her subjects.

"Aloha," she cried, "Aloha" . . . Then sitting down and disregarding the presence of the seamen and her attendants, she wept uncontrollably. There were journalists on the ship to see and report her every act; they recorded that when she reached the ship she remained alone on deck, and for the rest of the voyage spoke to nobody.

When the ship arrived in Honolulu the newspapers were filled with enthusiastic praise for the Princess. Every detail of the trip was printed and the Board of Health was severely criticized for its neglect of the colony. But Damien was the subject of a flood of glowing adjectives. Wrote the editor of the *Commercial Advertiser* (Sept. 24, 1881):

"But this lamentable history of the lepers, this gloomy page in the annals of Hawaii, is brightened and embellished above all by the devotedness and noble sacrifice of a kind-hearted man. This young priest, Damien by name, who has consecrated his life to the lepers, is the glory and boast of Hawaii. He resuscitates the saintly heroism of the bloody arenas of the ages of old; nay, he does even more. Would it not be a great favour to be thrown a prey to a wild beast rather than be condemnd to live in the poisonous atmosphere of a leper settlement? And Damien, the Soldier of Christ, has lived now several years in the midst of the banished lepers of Molokai! He is constantly in the midst of those suffering people, who live separated from the rest of human society as plague-stricken men whom the healthy dare not even approach, much less touch. He devotes himself entirely to their services, he dresses their wounds, and inspires them with confidence in their divine Master and with hope for a better life. Finally, when death arrives, he buries them with his own hands . . ."

Before the month was out, Msgr. Herman Koeckmann, titular Bishop of Alba, arrived in Honolulu to act as Coadjutor to the aging Bishop Maigret. This priest had served a number of years in the Islands as a pastor but had been consecrated to the higher rank in San Francisco. On his return to Honolulu, as was customary with such a dignitary, the representative of France, a Chargé d'Affaires in rank, donned his diplomatic uniform and conveyed him to the palace. The Princess Regent received them graciously and, when the court formalities of introduction and greeting had been concluded, spoke of Damien and asked the Bishop if he would undertake a mission to the priest on her behalf. On his assenting, she gave him a letter and a small flat leather box which contained the jewelled insignia of the Order of Kalakaua. The letter was addressed to Father Damien and read:

REVEREND SIR,

I desire to express to you my admiration of the heroic and distinguished service you are rendering to the most unhappy of my subjects; and to pay, in some measure, a public tribute to the devotion, patience and unbounded charity with which you give yourself to the corporal and spiritual relief of these unfortunate people, who are necessarily deprived of the affectionate care of their relations and friends.

I know well that your labors and sacrifices have no other motive than the desire to do good to those in distress; and that you look for no reward but from the great God, our sovereign Lord, who directs and inspires you. Nevertheless to satisfy my own earnest desire, I beg of you, Reverend Father, to accept the decoration of the Royal Order of Kalakaua, as a testimony of my sincere admiration for the efforts you are making to relieve the distress and lessen the sufferings of these afflicted people, as I myself had an occasion to see on my recent visit to the settlement.

I am,
Your friend,
LILIUOKALANI, Regent

Once again the Hawaiian press sent up a chorus of approval:

"Credit is due the Government (said the Advertiser) because it testifies its gratitude to this man, as Her Royal Highness, the Princess-Regent, has most justly and happily done in conferring on the saintly priest the order of Kalakaua. Honor then to the noble heart of the princess who has made so wise and worthy a use of her power in rewarding such self-devotion."

Altercations that arise from differences of religion or sect are ever delicate and difficult subjects to discuss; but following such recognition of the priest's work there was some resentment shown from a group who cloaked their envy under the guise of religion and who sought in every way to obstruct his mission and discredit him. Of them the Gazette wrote:

"We have yet another cause for satisfaction, in that the Regent has risen superior to the partisan prejudices of a petty clique, by thus rewarding merit without regard to any particular religious belief. This is that true liberty of thought which is a distinctive mark of our age. Men have learned to appreciate one another's merit, without having regard to religious opinion; they have learned to do away with those animosities and that lowness of spirit which are the marks of a narrow and uncultured intellect. We are proud today that the princess does not let herself be influenced by similar motives, and that, all zealous as she is for the Protestant cause, she does, none the less, distinguish that merit which is worthy of reward, even in those who hold different religious beliefs."

Much to his discomfort and before the interested eyes of his parishioners Damien was formally invested with the insignia of the decoration on the steps of his chapel at Kalawao by Bishop Koeckmann who placed the gold and scarlet ribbon around the priest's neck and read aloud the royal decree. Other than that it showed the Princess' favor Damien had no great interest in the bauble and sought to remove it as quickly as possible, giving as an excuse that its glitter went ill with the patches of his faded cassock. The Bishop sternly commanded him to wear it, but that night the medal was placed back in its box and there it remained, never to be seen again, until discovered after the priest's death.

More important to him than any medal was Liliuoka-lani's gracious letter. His hopes mounted high as he thought of how Governmental aid to the lepers could be spurred and increased under her patronage. In his happiness he disclosed many plans to the Bishop. All were of course connected with the condition of his lepers. He talked enthusiastically of the hospitals and orphanages that were to be conducted on a vast and scientific scale. He painted a picture of a settlement, indeed almost a principality, that would be under ecclesiastical rule like the larger monasteries and lazar houses of the middle ages.

Nuns would nurse the sick and teach the children. Monks would be trained as physicians and chemists, and other monks would attend to the more menial duties. Excepting for the lepers, there would be no place for laymen in this establishment, the workers would all be volunteers under Church discipline, sworn to remain among the lepers for life, without fear, without family ties and without any hope of earthly reward. Occupations and industries suitable to the strength and ability of the lepers were to be founded and in this haven of the future there was to be a laboratory where scientists and technicians could systematically study and fight the disease.

It was his dream, his ambition. He spoke of it with the fond warmth and enthusiasm that men feel for such visions.

Hope he might, and dream he did, but as the months passed, and then the years, the consciousness slowly came to him that the goodwill of Royalty does not necessarily mean the help of Governments. It is true that after the Regent's visit there was an improvement in the Board of Health's attitude towards the colony but to the priest who saw men die—sometimes only because of the conditions— almost every day, the efforts of the authorities seemed piti- fully insufficient against the picture of the efficient insti- tution his hopes had painted. The charity of the Nuns in Honolulu and his own work seemed of little account, sub- ject as they were to the vagaries of time and circumstance. His heart sank as he studied reports of the disease in India, China, South America and other parts of the world. It was the same depressing story of Hawaii: either the lepers were beggars and outcasts, shunned and loathed, or they were confined in the most primitive of "settlements" to be com- pletely forgotten by their more fortunate fellows.

Humanity in general seemed determined to ignore the existence of lepers. When, because of poverty, the priest was forced to deny a poor wretch the solace of an adequate bandage for his sores, he could not but think of the fine houses and splendid carriages of the officials who were apparently so indifferent to the needs of Molokai and yet who talked so convincingly, so cruelly, of budget limitations.

Dreams vanished and his hope turned to a disillusionment which flavored many of his actions. The pace of his work never slackened nor did his consideration for his charges lessen, but in his dealings with those outside the ranks of the lepers he became abruptly harsh in manner, quick to take offense, and quick to quarrel. Always impatient with the ways of officialdom, his wranglings with them now increased in number and vehemence. There were many times when it was he who, undoubtedly, was in the wrong.

Even fellow priests were not exempt from his ill-humor. With the consent of the Bishop, Father Andrew Burgermann moved to Kalaupapa in an effort to lighten some of Damien's burdens but after much disagreement with the priest, he was forced to resign and leave the settlement. He was a hard and courageous worker but Damien expected men to follow his own example which, from a physical standpoint alone, was almost impossible. Few men of ordinary caliber could be expected to slave day in and day out at the hard manual tasks that he accomplished. In 1882 another volunteer, Father Albert Montitor (who had accompanied Monseigneur Maigret on the first episcopal visit) arrived to assist at the colony. He, too, was soon indulging in altercations with the priest. Two years were the most he could endure and then once again Damien was alone (1884).

When no one came to replace Father Albert he petitioned the Bishop, stressing the need for an assistant. Now there was nobody who appreciated Damien's worth more than Msgr. Koeckmann but, disciplinarian as his position forced him to be, his reply was the cold comment:

"Father Albert would still be with him if he (Damien)

were a little more accommodating with his fellow-priests, and less of an autocrat."

This harsher side of him was revealed only to ordinary men, for his ill-temper never touched the lepers. To them he always remained the same, a kind father, sometimes stern perhaps, but always just and understanding and ready to help. No matter how violent his rages or how wrong his quarrels, it must be remembered that they were never motivated by selfishness. Whatever he did, he did for his lepers. Their life was his life; he had made it so since he first put foot on the island.

Then he had been a young man, splendid in health and burning with zeal, to whom no obstacle was too large to overcome. But now, after twelve years on Molokai, he seemed, to the interested eyes of a visiting official, "an embittered old man," undeniably devout and courageous, but soured with disappointment. This was in 1885 when he actually was only forty-five years old.

That same year, on the morning of the first Sunday in June, he was celebrating early Mass in the chapel at Kalawao with his customary fervor, chanting the Latin in his deep, steady voice and showing no other emotion than his usual devotion. In fact during the entire ritual of that morning he did nothing to indicate that the Mass might be different from the many he had celebrated before; the *Introit* was said and the *Gloria* was sung with spirit, genuflections were made with the requisite pomp, and the altar boys concluded that their priest was in the best of humors when, in stumbling over their responses, they received no frown.

It was a hot day. In the sultry, crowded interior, the congregation, all of whom were invalids in varying stages of the disease, probably welcomed the relaxation that comes with end of the Gospel. Perhaps, even, there were a few that, with a torpor induced by the heat, might have been inclined to drowsiness as the priest, standing before the altar, divested himself of chasuble and maniple in preparation for the sermon. But after he had advanced to the sanctuary rail (he had no pulpit), and began to talk, all signs of lethargy among his listeners quickly vanished. There was a sudden shocked stir, for instead of addressing them with the usual *My brethren*, he had said, slowly and significantly, *We lepers.* . . .

It was his way of telling them that he had contracted their disease.

CHAPTER XII

"Why don't you rest, Father Damien?" one of his parishioners asked.

"Rest?" he retorted, "it's no time to rest now, when there is so much left to do and my time is so short!"

No doubt was there as to whether he had the disease. A few months previous to his dramatic announcement, he had, while shaving, upset a kettle of boiling water on his bare foot; although the scalding liquid had seared his skin there had been no pain. Lack of sensibility is one of the first stages of leprosy, a symptom which he of course instantly recognized. Disturbing as this knowledge must have been, he nevertheless made no mention of it until Dr. Arning, a German physician, came to the settlement.

When the two men met on the beach and were introduced by an officer from the steamer, the doctor, who was an enthusiastic admirer of Damien's work, was astonished and chagrined to find the priest seemingly ignoring his proffered hand; surprise, however, gave way to concern when Damien, as they walked to the village, excused himself for his apparently unfriendly act by saying, in the most matter-of-fact manner, as though it were of little consequence, that he believed he had contracted leprosy.

The doctor made a careful diagnosis.

"I cannot bear to tell you," he said, "but what you say is true."

His distress was so evident at being forced to deliver such a terrible verdict that the priest assured him: "It is no shock to me for I have long felt sure of it."

Indeed from statements he made later it seems that for

some years previous to Arning's visit, certain symptoms, such as peculiar discolorations of his skin, had served to give him suspicions, which were strengthened by the incident of the boiling water and confirmed by Arning. Yet only twelve months before this diagnosis another physician, Dr. Mouritz of Honolulu, had come to the colony, but the priest made no effort to consult him although the doctor was to claim, in a document written in after years, that his suspicions had also been aroused because Damien's complexion had been of a copper hue: "A visible proof," he writes, "of the invasion of the destroyer."

Whether it was merely a deep sunburn that this medico saw or an actual effect of the disease, it is certain the deadly germs had been with Damien long before he announced it, for within three months after that time the effects of the disease were savagely visible. "His foot became entirely insensible and his right ear became swollen," (said he, when finally he wrote his report), "with a tubercular enlargement making the whole thing an immense affair. At the same time began the disfigurement of person in a general and marked manner . . ."

On every side there were dreadful examples of what his own fate was to be. The constant threat of an early and horrible death could not but intrude itself in his mind, yet his only worry was for his charges, a fear that his departure would mean the end of his reforms and a return to the ways of the earlier days of the settlement. "I would not," were his words to Dr. Arning, "have my health restored to me at the price of my having to leave the island and abandon my work here."

With astounding energy he embarked on new enterprises, and at both the chapels every day the sores of the more hopeless were washed and bandaged with the same meticulous care. He heard confessions, read the burial services, and, while his hands remained whole, continued to assist at the digging of the graves and the making of the coffins. Martyrdom might certainly be his, but he claimed no privileges. On the contrary he acted as though the coming of the disease was something to be welcomed, inasmuch as it removed the final barrier between him and his people. "We lepers," he had said, and the utterance of those two words was the seal of a bond that was as binding as an earthly link could be.

Perhaps he realized that the eyes of the entire settlement, and afterwards those of a far wider audience, were upon him, or perhaps it was the absolute certainty of his doom, but a new mood began to envelop him. Hitherto he had always been what is known as a serious man, but now he made it a point always to have a smile and to be cheerful on every occasion. Even the officials were not exempt from this new spirit. From this time onward their relations with him, though perhaps not completely harmonious, were to be more agreeable than they had ever been in the past. No longer was his readiness for hostility so pronounced. Whatever his thoughts were, his actions showed a lessening of the bitterness that had tinged his latter years. Where, with his sick charges, he had been kind to the children, nursing, feeding and teaching them, he now joined in their games and it became no uncommon sight to see a dozen of the pitiable urchins frolicking around the priest, shouting and laughing, as he walked from his labors to his hut. Formerly with his hammer and chisel he had made only the most practical of articles but now, if he had an hour's leisure, it would be passed by fashioning a crude toy. And in Honolulu the Sisters received requests for dolls and doll's clothing.

In writing from the settlement he made no mention of having contracted the disease. Rumors however reached the Bishop who, after receiving the necessary permission from the authorities, wrote to the priest and bade him come to Honolulu. His answer was Damien's first written mention of his fate:

"I cannot come (he wrote) for leprosy has attacked me.

163

There are signs of it on my left cheek and ear, and my eyebrows are beginning to fall. I shall soon be quite disfigured. I have no doubt whatever about the nature of my illness, but I am calm and resigned and very happy in the midst of my people . . . I daily repeat from my heart, 'Thy Will be done.' "

On receipt of this letter the Bishop lost no time in ordering Damien to report to the branch hospital at Kakaako (Honolulu). It was a command that the priest dreaded for he had no wish to leave his people; he made excuses and sent lengthy reasons as to why he should remain on Molokai. But his superior was firm. After as many delays as he could dare, Damien gloomily set about making preparations for the journey and assured his parishioners that he would be back within a few weeks.

There was a reason for the Bishop's persistence. A new treatment was being tried, and apparently with some success, by a Japanese doctor at the Branch Hospital. Known as the Goto method, it was a complicated and tedious process of baths, massages, and injections of certain drugs. While it was not, nor was it claimed to be, an actual cure, there were some instances where it had both relieved and arrested the sickness.

The scene of these experiments, the Branch Hospital, was a prison-like place where lepers, after the first symptoms of their ailment had been detected, were supposed to wait for shipment to Molokai. Actually, because of the general fear of the settlement and because of the muddled and ever-changing policies of the Board of Health, many remained permanently and never saw the Island. Although nominally under Government rule and control, it had been conducted since 1884 by a courageous group of Franciscan nuns whose arrival in the Islands for such work was the result of a campaign originated by Damien.

As far back as 1873, a month after he had landed in Molokai for the first time, he had written: "If I had here a dozen hospital Sisters, they could render very great service." Every time he saw the Bishop he mentioned the same need but, as can be readily understood, it was hard for that dignitary to make an official request for women to volunteer for such a place. Then, too, there was always the loud opposition certain to be voiced from the bigoted anti-Catholic element if more nuns were brought to the Islands. However, the Bishop did not oppose the scheme but intimated that the proposal should first come from other than ecclesiastical sources, before receiving the seal of his approval.

Damien talked with various officials, at first meeting with no success because of the usual cry of "expense," until in 1883 a Dr. Fitch, who was a member of the Board of Health, wrote to Msgr. Koeckmann, mentioning that he was familiar with the conditions in both Molokai and the Branch Hospital and that in both places the leper's lot was pitiable . . . "their friends are no longer concerned about them; they are left to themselves (reads his letter) in a wretched state until the end of their sad existence arrives. Not a friend is near to console them in their last hour, when death with its terrors is ready to seize upon its prey. I am mistaken, there are two priests—Father Damien who has worked among them for nearly ten years and discharges his noble task to perfection, and good Father Albert, who has assisted him for more than a year now.

"But the devotedness of these two men is not sufficient for seven hundred lepers, and sometimes more; we want also women to render assistance to the infirm. I have therefore taken the liberty of proposing to the Board of Health to consider with your Lordship whether there would be no possibility of obtaining twenty-five hospital nuns to assist these poor patients.

"I am a Protestant, as you know; but I am fully acquainted, from personal experience in California, with the merit of these devoted women. They, more than any others, are capable of seeing to the proper cooking of the

165

food, of keeping the children tidy, and above all, of teaching men an esteem for virtue and the practice of chastity.

"I have broached the subject to several of the most influential of the Protestant creed. They are unanimous in recognizing the excellence of the work, and wish it a complete success. As soon as your Lordship is able to make known to me the approaching arrival of Sisters, I confidently declare that I shall find among my fellow-citizens the necessary means to procure them suitable lodging and a permanent home. The Protestants, I have no doubt, will themselves generously contribute to this execution of this project."

Victory it was for the Catholic missionaries who but forty-four years previously had needed a French frigate to protect them. Still the Bishop demurred. The letter was an impressive acknowledgment of his priests' work but to him who knew well the vagaries of Hawaiian politics the request did not yet have enough of an official flavor. This quickly came in a letter from Mr. Walter Gibson, Minister of Foreign Affairs and a person of great influence with the King.

"My Lord (he wrote), as I am aware that eminent institutions of charity, such as this country needs, abound in the Catholic Church, and as I feel assured that your representation would be all influential, I make an appeal, and offer an invitation through you, to sisters of charity of your church, to come to the help of the sick of this country; and I doubt not I may proffer to them in advance the profound obligation and gracious recognition of their Majesties, the thanks of His Majesty's government and the blessings of the Hawaiian people. . . ."

This last letter satisfied the Bishop, with the result that the following November seven nuns of the Franciscan Order, all volunteers for work among the lepers, landed from the steamer "Mariposa" which had brought them from San Francisco. They were headed by Mother Marianne Kopp, a tall, handsome woman who, like Damien, was to display remarkable qualities of piety and courage combined with initiative and good sense. To their amazement the startled Sisters, all of whom were either of Irish or German descent, were greeted with royal honors. The bells of the city rang and crowds gathered at the steamer wharf to roar enthusiastic "Alohas." The Queen sent four royal carriages, complete with brightly uniformed footmen and grooms, to transport them to the Cathedral where the Bishop awaited surrounded by his staff. The next day the Sisters were taken to the Palace and presented to Her Majesty who was curious to see these white women who aspired to the same fate as Damien. She had heard of their vows of poverty and, when Mother Marianne shook hands with her, she, much to the nun's embarrassment, left a hundred-dollar bill in her hand.

Meanwhile the Board of Health, apparently acting on the principle that charity should begin at home, decided that the Sisters should not go to Molokai, but should commence their work at the Branch Hospital which institution, in all truth, was sorely in need of their services. In fact, conditions there were almost as bad as those that had beset the lepers in the early days of Molokai, and the only excuse the place had for the name hospital was that the inmates were grievously ill. Actually it was a collection of poorly built wooden buildings, set in a sea-bordered salt marsh, and surrounded by high palisaded walls, around which the water would flood at high tide. It looked like a species of filthy primitive prison. The few attendants, monstrously inefficient, who were in charge, had adopted the attitude of jailers towards the lepers, even to the extent of providing cells for solitary confinement punishment. The kitchen was a stoveless shed, in which a few fire pits had been dug, and was presided over by lepers whose sores were rarely covered with a bandage. There were no sanitary or drainage arrangements of even the most elementary kind, and the stench of the foul place was a warning that persisted for considerable distance.

Into this place the seven nuns entered and took residence. Their first six months there, among some two hundred lepers of all ages, of both sexes, and of varying dispositions, is almost the same story of Damien's arrival at Kalawao, except that he was a man and they were but women. Cleanliness was their first goal. Every corner of the establishment was washed and scrubbed and fumigated, and arrangements made to keep it so before fresh problems were attacked. Of course, there were the usual oppositions. Once or twice even violence was attempted. But the calm wisdom of Mother Marianne proved equal to all occasions and gradually the institution took on the semblance of an actual hospital.

More nuns arrived, the Government increased the financial grants, the citizens of Honolulu sent generous gifts, and several doctors from the town began to make regular weekly visits. Among them was the one of whom Mother Marianne reported to her Superior that "We have now a doctor from Japan, who makes the treatment of leprosy a specialty. He comes to the Hospital daily and treats seventy patients; all are doing wonderfully well. He gives hot medicated baths twice daily and medicine before and after meals. The doctor's treatment increases our work but we do it cheerfully when we see such a good effect. Several patients are so much improved that the doctor thinks of discharging them soon, which is something quite unheard of in the history of leprosy."

When Damien came to the hospital for the purpose of receiving the new treatment it was a big event in the life of the nuns. He was their hero, the man whose example had brought them across the seas from the tranquillity of their cloisters, and with the utmost care they prepared for his coming. Sister Antonella Murphy whitewashed a room especially for him. Mother Marianne hung her own crucifix on the wall. Each of the other Sisters contributed something, holy pictures and patchwork quilts, things from home that were particularly precious to them who had so little. For the first time in years the priest was to feel the luxury of sheets.

By the time he arrived the disease had thoroughly distorted his face. His nose had swollen, his ears were misshapen, and his complexion was purplish-red in color. The Sisters wept when they saw him and with solicitous and tender care waited upon him, anticipating, whenever possible, his every wish and want, exerting every effort to make his stay comfortable.

Damien was not used to being treated as an invalid and such a passive role was hard for his energetic nature to accept. The constant attendance and the anxious fluttering of skirts that attended his every movement served only to make him uneasy. It was a torture for him to sit long inactive hours, as the treatment called for, in the hot baths. A cloud of gloom enveloped his restless spirit. He continually fretted about the affairs of his people at Molokai. No treatment could possibly be of any use to him while he was in such a state of mind. Soon it became obvious to all that he would have to be allowed his wish and be returned to the settlement.

So, within two weeks after he landed in Honolulu, he was on a steamer again, bound back to Molokai. Mother Marianne escorted him on board and remained until the ship sailed to bid him farewell. These two, who in so many respects were alike, appreciated each other's worth to fullest degree. One thing accomplished by his sojourn at the hospital was that he had convinced her the Sisters were urgently needed at the settlement, particularly for the children. This matter was the subject of a last anxious discussion before the ship sailed. They both knew that it would take considerable pleading and maneuvering with the Board of Health, as that lofty body had many other plans for the Sisters' future activities. A blast from the ship's whistle intruded upon their talk and a gong was beaten

169

along the deck. It was time for Mother Marianne to go ashore. From the wharf she said her final farewell and once again made reassurances that he would be soon seeing some of the Sisters on Molokai. Hawsers splashed the water and the steamer pulled slowly away from the wharf as the priest made his reply.

"Hurry," he cried, "there is not much time, you know."

She nodded and smiled and waved and tried gallantly to pretend that she did not know he was speaking of his death. But it was a dismal departure. The sadness of the moment was intensified by the wailing of a contingent of fellow and unwilling passengers, all lepers, who were being transported to the colony. To the sound of their unceasing dirge the priest, standing by the after rail, watched the crowded colorful harbor, then the rich panorama of the island recede.

The lacework of peaks and mountain tops rising to the clouds and forming a gigantic palette of lovely colors, splashed haphazard but divinely, had been his first view of Honolulu. There was no doubt in his mind, as he gazed at the beautiful picture, that it would be his last. Gradually, as distance lengthened and night came, all that he could see had faded to a distant shadow. He still kept his vigil, standing at the stern, staring into the darkness.

It was there that he was found by the captain, a tall sunburnt giant, American in nationality; the same man who had refused to allow the priest to come aboard his ship to confess to the Bishop, but who now was carrying a decanter and two glasses and seemed anxious to please.

"Father," he said, and his words came awkwardly and apologetically, "I thought you might like to have a little wine with me."

In the dim light the priest recognized him. He shook his head. "You forget," he told him, "I am a leper."

The other made a gesture as though this fact did not disturb him, then in a low voice paid what was for him the

170

highest tribute that could be rendered. He said that Damien was the bravest man he had ever met.

Damien made no reply to this unexpected statement, nor did the other seek to amplify it. For an hour they stayed there, leaning against the rail that trembled with the vibration of the propeller, lost in the shadows of the poop, both remaining and respecting the silence as though feeling their smallness under the vast star sprinkled arch of the tropic night, staring back upon the vanishing furrow of the steamer's wake, absorbed in their thoughts, in the mystery of their being. The throbbing of the engines, the distant occasional clang of a shovel in the stokehold, the perpetual lament of the doomed passengers, created a strange sad harmony that was hard to disturb with mere conversation. But the seaman had a conscience to ease, suddenly declaring the confessional incident was a memory that had always served to make him unhappy and that he had long waited this opportunity of expressing sorrow and asking forgiveness.

"It is given," said the priest, simply.

The captain still had something to say, although the words came hard. He swept an arm against the splendid immensity of sea and sky as though it were an irrefutable document. "When one sees that all the time, one cannot deny *somebody* is in control of everything but . . ." he hesitated for a moment, then concluded quickly, "Father, I don't know much about it."

The tone of his voice was both a plea and a question that Damien had to answer. They walked to the bridge. There by the dim light of the shaded chart-table lamp he sought to tell something of his faith to the attentive seaman.

It was a strange yet fitting background for such a conversation. The severe accouterments of navigation glittering in the shadows; the silent, still figure of the native helmsman standing but a few paces away, brooding over the polished brightness of the binnacle; the motionless mate of the watch, propped on the opposite wing of the bridge, staring into the horizon, a vigilant silhouette against a curtain of stars that shifted slowly with the roll of the ship.

Midnight came, eight bells were struck by the quartermaster, new men came to the bridge and changed places with the unostentatious ceremony of the sea, but the low murmur of the quiet voice continued, uninterrupted, until dawn, when the anchorage was sighted. Above everything else, Damien was, at all times, the missionary.

CHAPTER XIII

His mother was still alive, but was very old, and he had been reluctant to write and startle her with the news of his sickness. But after the journey to Honolulu the story soon reached the newspapers of the world. At Tremeloo his family read a sensationally written account which declared the priest's flesh was in shreds and that his hands and feet had decayed to stumps. The shock proved too great for his mother and the next day, after seeing the terrifying story, with rosary clasped devoutly in her hands and with her eyes fixed on a photograph of Damien, she died.

The news of her death, relayed by Pamphile, found the priest not entirely unprepared. Earlier in the year, hearing of her weakened condition, he had written: "Eighty-two years of a pious and laborious life cannot be far from the reward of eternal repose. I have no doubt that she is preparing . . . for a holy death. Your frequent visits will supply for my absence; take care to assure her that I always remember her at the altar."

Pamphile had long wished to assist at Molokai and now, after the death of Madame de Veuster, he redoubled his efforts in this direction. For some reason his Superiors refused to accede. Both brothers were profoundly disappointed but Damien offered the consolation:

"Our good God has fixed your residence in our native country, that your special mission might be to labour for the salvation of our family and others of our countrymen, as mine has been clearly traced out among the lepers. . . .

173

The best, both for you and for me, will be to leave it entirely to the ecclesiastic authorities to decide whether I shall have the consolation of having as my fellow laborer a brother to whom I am indebted after God that I was chosen for mssions. You understand me, I know, without my saying all I think."

There were others, however, with the same hopes who were more successful than Pamphile. When the news of Damien becoming a leper reached them, four men, two of whom were priests, and who lived in different parts of the world, became determined to come to Molokai and help the priest in his work. All four were to realize their ambitions and were to arrive on the island before the death of the man whose example had inspired them. The first to come, Joseph Dutton, was to be the one who, before all others, became Damien's friend and confidant and who was to remain and work at the settlement for forty-four years.

Dutton's life, before he came to the Islands, reads like a romantic novel, containing all the adventurous elements that go to make such a work. He had been both soldier and monk, he had been the victim of an unhappy love affair; in fact there are some who say that the stories "The White Cowl" and "The Garden of Allah" are based on his experiences.

Originally his name had been Ira Dutton but when he became a Catholic in 1883, on his fortieth birthday, he changed it to Joseph. Like Damien's, his birthplace was a small village (Stowe, in the state of Vermont). There the similarity ceases. While the priest was of peasant blood, Dutton was the son of an American pioneer family, transplanted landed gentry from England, whose ancestors had fought at Hastings with the Conqueror. His parents were a kindly and considerate pair, and his childhood and adolescence were pleasantly uneventful. After some years spent at various correct academies, at manhood he decided that he might try his hand at journalism; but by this time it was 1861, and guns at Fort Sumter were heralding the commencement of the Civil War.

Lincoln issued a proclamation calling for volunteers and young Dutton promptly enlisted. The military life came easy to him. When the day arrived for his regiment to leave the town he records that it was: "an exciting time. The streets were lined with cheering crowds, bands playing, flags flying . . ." The traditional picture was completed by a childhood sweetheart who rushed from the crowd as the warriors swung by and pressed a tintype of herself into the young soldier's hand. He was soon to discover that war had its grimmer moments, but he proved a good soldier. Two years later, as a lieutenant, one of his generals referred to him as "the handsomest fellow I ever met, and one of the bravest and best officers in the Army."

He seems to have enjoyed the war, this most tragic but romantic conflict of brother against brother, blue against gray. The hard-riding cavalry raids, the daring sallies into enemy territory, the desperate charges, the calm evenings of summer bivouacs, the shrill of pipe and drum, all went to make pleasant fare for him. And there was even one adventurous interlude connected with a woman spy when the business of stolen maps and changing passwords, flavored with the magical spice of a petticoat, took on an added charm. Widows might weep and infantrymen might curse but there is no denying that at twenty-two years of age it must be a glorious feeling to command a troop of horses, to swing to the saddle as bugles lilt, to point a saber and cry "Charge!" Comrades might die, but when a young man paraded to the music of rattling drums and jingling harness and shouted "Eyes Right!" to his men and swept a sword in proud salute as generals and fluttering standards were passed in review, the sacrifice of friends seemed not in vain, death was not to be feared.

Dutton was always to remain the soldier. Even as an old man on Molokai, engaged in the peaceful pursuit of nursing lepers, he would cast a soldierly eye at the high hills and appraise their worth as fortifications. Many a plan did he draw of these imaginary battlements. When in later years a flag staff was erected at the colony, it became his particular pleasure to see that the national colors were raised and lowered with all the niceties of martial etiquette. If any unfortunate persons neglected to bare their head or stand at attention during the ritual of this solemn moment, a scathing rebuke, administered in the loudest and most approved parade-ground voice, would quickly inform them of the error of their ways.

He was not wounded during the Civil War but this good fortune seems not, at the time, to have given him any great sense of religious responsibility. He lived the usual life of his fellows. When the regiment was at rest, he drank hard and gambled heavily, nor is there any reason to believe that he missed his share of feminine company. The sweetheart of his adolescent years, she who had pressed the tintype into his hand as he marched to war, seems to have been soon forgotten; but his heart was given to none in particular until a month or so after the conclusion of the conflict when, at a ball given in honor of the regiment, he met a glamorous young creature before whose charms he made a complete and instant surrender. It was a pretty and sure scene for romance, music and candlelight and bare shoulders, the dashing young officer in his blue and gold, she in her wide skirts and curls and demurely calling him "Sir" while her dark eyes danced invitingly over the rim of her fan.

Of course they fell in love. They became engaged, but his life still continued to follow the uneven, incredible lines of a popular novel of that very period. For when he announced the happy news of his betrothal to his fellow officers, there were averted faces and sidelong looks and the congratulations that came were weak and forced. The young lady, it appeared, had a "past," uniforms had always found her gracious, too gracious. When a well meaning

176

Major tried to tell young Dutton so, there were many angry words, almost a duel. After this disagreeable incident his comrades let him alone and he had his way and was married. She promptly broke his heart with not one but a series of flaunted infidelities. The wretched hopeful tenacity of his infatuation made him endure these miseries for about a year. Then she, after incurring enormous debts, eloped to New York with another man.

It was a good riddance but he took it hard. The immediately succeeding years form the portion of his life of which he was to be so ashamed and concerning which little is known, save that he became a drunkard and sank to the depths of habitual dissipation. This period lasted in all about ten years. Then gradually he seems to have climbed from the associations of his despair to his former station in life. He had long left the army. Now he rejoined the Government service. By the time the year 1883 had arrived we find him in Memphis, Tennessee, a most respectable and eligible bachelor. A few years before he had divorced his wife on the charges of "adultery with sundry persons on divers occasions." She treated the divorce as she had treated the letters in which he had begged her to return; she ignored the proceedings entirely. The year following the divorce saw her death. It must be stressed that there was no connection between the two events; she, who knew so many men, seems to have completely forgotten him after the brief period of their marriage.

In the Southern town of Memphis, Dutton, the Northern officer, was "accepted" in the best houses. He seems to have created quite a stir among the local belles, who were intrigued rather than daunted by the rumors that surrounded his unfortunate marriage. His popularity was all the more remarkable, a triumph of tact and graciousness, when it is remembered that his residence in town was due to the fact that his were the disagreeable duties of representing the victorious Government's interests in settling and defending claims brought against the Union troops by private citizens.

One of the town's most prominent hostesses and one whose house was apparently somewhat of a cultural rendezvous was a Mrs. Benedict Semmes, wife of a former Confederate officer, still staunchly Southern in sympathy; her cousin had commanded the warship "Alabama." Yet, despite political and indeed religious differences, for they were devout Catholics, both husband and wife became Dutton's closest friends. It was to Mrs. Semmes that he first voiced his intention of becoming a Catholic. "I told her (he says) all my past life, and what I had in mind. For a while she tried to dissuade me from the step I thought of taking, saying that she doubted whether my disposition was fitted for it." She finally introduced him to a well known Dominican, Fr. Joseph Kelly, who prepared him for baptism. Then, suddenly, without any announcement or any explanation, he resigned his official position and vanished from the town, leaving a chorus of gossip that waxed strong indeed when, a month or so later, it was rumored that the dashing officer, the fashionable cavalier, had immured himself behind the walls of a monastery.

It was true. He had selected the grim confines of a Trappist Abbey to be the scene of his retirement from the world; an abbey belonging to the same stern Order whose austere life had attracted Damien in student days. "Though I knew it was a severe discipline," Dutton explains, "yet it seemed to be what I needed at the time." It was undoubtedly severe; hard manual labor and perpetual silence, except at prayer, poverty and humility were and are the chief rules of the Order. Every morning, regardless of weather or season, the monks rose from their hard pallets at the hour of two to chant the morning Office, then, after a few hours' rest, to the fields where they worked until sunset, pausing only for the prayers. Silence, always silence, is their rule. To emphasize the gloom, close by the walls of the Abbey an open grave yawns, ready to receive the next monk who should die. The ceremonies that surround the burial service of a Trappist are just as grim as those that rule his life. The corpse is placed on ashes that are strewn, cross-shaped, on the cold stone floor of the chapel. There the other monks can see and be reminded that theirs will be a similar fate. After the requiem has been sung, the body, coffinless, is taken and lowered into the waiting grave; another pit is then dug, to await the next death.

Dutton entered and remained as a novice in the Order, that is to say he never took any vows and he was free to leave at any time he so wished.

"It seems well," he writes, "to put this matter on record. I am not under vows—have never made any, not even in the twenty months when I lived with the Trappists. I did take with Fr. Damien a yearly vow to the Catholic Mission at Molokai, but when the Brothers and Sisters came, I stopped doing this. I am not and never have been a Brother in the sense used by religious orders. I am just a common, everyday layman. Various designations have been added by good friends in correspondence, such as Father, Brother, Venerable, etc.; but I sign simply Joseph Dutton."

Near the end of his stay at the monastery there occurred the incident that is flavored with the touch of the dramatic so characteristic of his entire life. One morning while cutting grass on the field that bordered the highway he was startled by a feminine scream; almost immediately a runaway horse galloped by, throwing the rider, a young woman, almost at Dutton's feet. She was unconscious and he did what was, under the circumstances, the most practical thing to do; he carried her to a nearby schoolhouse; assisted the teacher in reviving her and then, after receiving her words of gratitude, departed to make a report to his superiors. It was an incident that many people have thought was responsible for his leaving the Abbey, and it was a supposition always to annoy him. He left the Trappists, and on the best of terms with them, solely because he felt that a more active life was more desirable, in his case, than the contemplative and routine existence of the monastery.

Remaining convinced that his destiny should be directed along penitential lines he began to search for a scene that would be suitable to his nature. Eventually this quest brought him to the library of the Redemptorist House, New Orleans, where one day he chanced to see an account of Father Damien and Molokai. As he read the heroic story he knew he would not have to look any further. He had found his vocation.

CHAPTER XIV

There were practical reasons, such as the reception of newcomers and the acceptance of stores, why Damien should be on the beach when a steamer dropped anchor off either of the settlement's two landings. He considered it as being one of the more pleasant of his tasks, for like many landsmen, the sea and ships that sailed it held a lingering fascination for him whom circumstances had confined to one horizon. Sea lore acquired under Captain Geerken's tutelage on the voyage from Belgium was never forgotten. Always he retained an eye for those nautical details which to the experienced gaze makes ships as varied and as individual as the appearances of men are to other men. The most ordinary of schooners had to visit the island for but a few hours and the next time her hull passed by those shores the priest would, from afar, instantly recognize and name her by the rake of a mast or the cut of a sail, the height of the poop or length of a boom. The intricacies of a steamer's superstructure were easily decipherable to him. It was with genuine pleasure and intense interest that he would watch the routine evolutions of a ship coming to anchor, the shouted commands, the rattle of machinery, the lowering of the boats, the anticipatory thrill that perhaps the vessel had brought letters from Belgium or a message from the Bishop. These things comprised a great sport for him, sitting on and watching from the beach.

After his return from Honolulu he continued this practice, although the disease had crippled his legs so that he could no longer negotiate the short distance on foot but was forced to use a ramshackle horse-drawn conveyance which was the gift of a non-leprous farmer from the opposite side of the island.

He was at his usual post of observation, a cluster of rocks on the beach, on the morning that saw the arrival of Dutton. As he watched the tall white man, obviously not a leper, swing his belongings from the deck of the steamer into the waiting lifeboat, his curiosity was naturally aroused. Visitors were rare enough at the settlement. A visitor with kitbags that betokened a lengthy stay was unheard of. As the sailors in the lifeboat strained at the oars, Dutton, on his part stared eagerly at the man on the shore, the face stained by the sun and so cruelly misshapen by the disease, the ill-fitting, patched cassock, the large and flaping, ludicrous hat of native manufacture, the pathetic figure, so easily recognizable, of the man whose life he had come to emulate.

The boat grated on the sand and the American stepped ashore to meet the priest. While the latter surveyed him curiously, Dutton briefly explained his ambition and position and stated that he wished no remuneration (during the long years that followed he never received as much as a single penny for his services, although several times a grateful government offered him a salary; indeed because of a legacy he was able to give away monies exceeding $10,000). He had credentials, letters of consent and approval from Bishop Koeckmann and the Board of Health, which Damien, staring shortsightedly through his thick lenses, scanned closely and slowly. Ecclesiastical and civil power might both be enthusiastic, but if the priest experienced any feelings of elation over the arrival of a sorely needed helper, he did not at first show it. Perhaps he doubted the ability of this gentlemanly individual to stand the hardships of the settlement, for after mentioning some of the worst conditions he asked: "Are you willing to make a vow that you will stay here for at least a year?"

"I am," was the reply.

Even this answer left Damien noncommittal at the moment, but with the inexplicable sympathy that breeds friendship at first sight, he rapidly warmed to the calm personality of his new assistant when they went on a tour of inspection through the two villages. As Dutton calmly and unflinchingly gazed upon each successive horror, the priest instinctively seemed to know, without any superfluity of words, that at last here was someone who would understand him, who would work with him in harmony and accord. In the twilight of a fast ebbing life Damien was to learn that he had found the most precious of human gifts; the jewel of friendship, something that, beyond the cordiality of his Bishop and the relationship of his lepers, had hitherto been alien to him.

Except for their spiritual beliefs and devotion to the sick, the two men were so utterly unlike in every respect that it seems strange they should become such staunch friends. Perhaps the very differences that marked their individual characters were the balancing influences that kept them in harmony. Damien, as his death approached, was to engage himself in a fever of activity that became almost frantic. With the inroads of disease giving him the same weaknesses as extreme age he, many times because of a failing memory, would leave unfinished a task to commence a new one; and the unfinished task would be sure to be completed by the faithful and tactful Dutton who, following behind, would carefully attack all problems with a methodical carefulness born of his army training; a schooling he never forgot. Always was he the officer, neat and trim in appearance and, so unlike Damien, extremely orderly in his quarters with blankets rolled and accouterments packed as though in perpetual readiness for the inspection of a visiting general.

Their first day together was busy with talk. Plans were discussed and a division of the work made. Dutton was to take care of the two churches and to assist, although he doubted his worthiness, the priest at Mass. As the latter's hands were rapidly becoming too swollen to be of such use, it was also agreed that the newcomer should gradually assume the unpleasant duties of dressing and washing the sores of the lepers at the hospital.

As the day ended and the heat went before the coolness of the evening, the two sat in front of the priest's hut which time had covered with a vine of honeysuckle. They watched the sky darken, then lighten again with the luminous gleam of a tropic night. The darknesses of the surrounding foliage became pale tapestries, silver-tipped with light. Damien, with the mood of a veteran pioneer upon him, puffed his pipe and pointed out the silhouette of the *pandanus* tree under which he had spent his first nights on the island. As his guest listened with grave attention, he talked of those times and of his hopes and prayers, and he painted a vivid picture of the great monastic institution which was his dream.

"You are the first of the Brothers to arrive," he told his listener with a smile. From then on Dutton was always Brother Joseph to the priest. There was other conversation too, and as the months went by, and the friendship grew and the priest learned the worth of his assistant, he began to have hopes that Dutton would be his successor in every respect.

"You should," he suggested one evening, "become a priest."

To his surprise Dutton emphatically refused to entertain such a thought but as he gave no reason, the strong willed Damien persisted in trying to change his mind. There could be no doubt, he thought, as to Dutton's piety, and concluded it might be the scholastic requirements that daunted him.

"You were an officer. Your education is good enough," he urged. "The Latin will come easily. Look at me, a peasant boy, and I learned quickly enough."

He told of his lessons with Pamphile. Dutton, thoroughly perturbed and obviously wishing to finish the subject, replied that it was not a question of education but of his fitness.

This answer puzzled Damien. He knew Dutton's object in coming to Molokai was a matter of self-imposed penance to atone for something that had happened in his former life; but, reasoned the priest, whatever the error or misdeeds were, they belonged to the past and had undoubtedly been erased in the confessional. Besides, he could not believe his friend had ever been guilty of any really great evil. With a tenacity that was so typical of him when he believed he was doing good, he kept at his persuasions for a period that lasted several months, with an insistence which was to make the unhappy Dutton refer to the entire incident as one of the hardest trials of his life, and which finally was to force him to reveal to Damien his actual reasons for objecting to taking Orders. It was a confidence he was never again to reveal to any other man. Whatever those reasons were, they were sufficient to cause the priest to desist from his urgings. After the explanation, Dutton was never to mention the subject again.

Another year came; the work went on. Damien was becoming accustomed to the luxury of an assistant. Each evening the laborers met and discussed the incidents of the day, the plans for the morrow. The lepers still came to serenade with the priest at the evening meal but they did not stay as late as formerly and, after their departure, he would with considerable difficulty, for his sight was getting weaker, now, read his breviary by the light of an oil lamp while Dutton would occupy himself busily with month-old newspapers in which he took a great interest. For although he had isolated himself from the world, he remained a keen observer of the actions of his fellowmen and of the comedies and tragedies of contemporary history.

Enough was happening that year to excite the imagination of an ex-soldier. In his own country Karl Marx was being read for the first time, strikes were assuming ugly proportions, and, to the harsh tune of gunfire, troops were helping harassed police struggle with the recalcitrant

Knights of Labor whose more conservative members were to form that very year the American Federation of Labor. If these troubles were not enough, President Cleveland and Secretary of State Bayard were exchanging coldly formal notes with the British Government, concerning the seizing by Her Majesty's ships of American fishing vessels while sailing in Canadian waters. But Her Majesty's ministers remained loftily undisturbed, being particularly complacent that year, for it was the Jubilee, the fiftieth anniversary of the Queen's reign, and on the whole the Empire, despite the petty incidents with the Americans and usual muttering from the inconsiderate Irish, was flourishing and growing too. Zululand was annexed that May, British rule in Burma formally acknowledged, and at distant Sarawak a romantic white Rajah, who was eyeing the Dutch nervously, was informed that he could soon expect the stability of Her Majesty's protection. In the Mediterranean, Italian and English officers toasted each other with enthusiastic speeches as a new pact of friendship was signed between their governments; the same treaty was toasted further north by Bismarck who, at the same time, frowning at the flirtings of France and Russia, was increasing the German army by forty thousand men.

Such events on the world's stage, seen from the perspective of remote Molokai, were of intense interest to Dutton who would have liked to discuss them with the priest. As has been seen, the latter was rarely communicative on matters that did not concern the settlement and the lepers, although when an account of the pageantry surrounding the Jubilee of Queen Victoria was read to him he was moved to mention that soon it would be the Jubilee of the Pope and that he would have liked to see the Vatican and the Holy Father before he died.

Another priest came to the settlement about this time. He can hardly be classed as a helper, for although he tried desperately to be of assistance he was a leper, suffering terribly in the last stages of the disease, and his stay was not for long. His name was Father Gregoire Archambeaux. He was a Frenchman who had contracted the malady upon one of the more distant islands of the south Pacific.

Damien, whose own condition was not much better, received him most hospitably and did his best to make his lot more agreeable. For a few Sundays this other priest was able to celebrate Mass at the chapel at Kalaupapa while Damien officiated at Kalawao; two leper priests leading their leper congregations to a divine consolation in a remarkable exhibition of their faith.

But Molokai was only to know Father Archambeaux for two months. By the end of that time he was absolutely incapacitated and near death. As he had great confidence in a certain doctor at Honolulu, he was, at his own request, put aboard the steamer and carried back to the Branch Hospital where, despite the efforts of his physician friend and the solicitude of Mother Marianne and the other Sisters, he died a short time afterwards.

By all rules Damien at this time should have been dead too but, with the stubbornness that was so much a part of him, he seemed to thrust away the final day; not because he feared the end, but because he thought the colony could not yet spare his presence. "There is so much left to do" was still the motto that governed his existence. The echo of his hammer, although his hands were almost too rotted to hold the tool, could still be heard every day.

His building activities had never ceased. Since Dutton's arrival a new community kitchen had been constructed; an establishment for medicated baths, the same Goto treatment the priest had tried at the Branch Hospital, had been erected. His favorite enterprise, the Home for leper children, had been enlarged.

But he was not satisfied. As he crossed the threshold of his last year, the high standards set by his restless eager mind, the same standards that had served to make him feel that even his most prodigious accomplishments were never enough, goaded him into a whirl of frantic endeavor as astonishing as it was frightening to those about him. It did not seem physically possible that his body, now pitifully shrunken and emaciated, could obey the regime set by that driving indomitable spirit. His fingers merged with his knuckles into ulcerous sores, raw, swollen, and huge. The bridge of his nose collapsed entirely. Completely blind in one eye, he was slowly losing the sight of the other. He tottered as he walked. In the chapel his people watched with agonized suspense when he celebrated Mass, for sometimes in bending low over the altar, still faithfully trying to follow the prescribed ritual, it seemed as though he would never raise head and shoulders again, so weak had he become.

"There is so much left to do." A horizon of achievement continued to beckon to him. A new chapel was planned and at the hospital a new building commenced. In vain Dutton begged him to desist, to rest. His only answer was "Off I am, Brother Joseph!" and although his pace was sometimes but a stagger, off he would go, to be followed by his worrying but ever faithful assistant. He lived on, but it did not seem possible. The disease was attacking him in all the senses, even his throat cankered until his voice became nothing more than a hoarse whisper. The days, the weeks, the months dragged by. His sky was darkening. Death had claimed his body but he would not die. His affairs, and that meant the affairs of his people, were not yet in order. Then as the year (1888) matured, his course was unexpectedly made easier by the arrival, all within a few months of each other, of no less than six helpers! Three men and three women. Not many surely, but to Damien who had been so long alone, it seemed like a regiment of Good Samaritans.

First to land at the settlement was Father Lambert Conrardy, who had been a missionary priest among the Indians of Oregon. After him came a Christian brother from Australia, Brother James, a tall, auburn-haired giant of an Irishman, who, the moment he had heard of Molokai in Sydney, had boarded a steamer. Next was Father Wendelin Moellers, a priest of the same Order as Damien. His arrival was the result of a circular letter sent by Bishop Koeckmann to the Catholic clergy of the Hawaiian Islands in which he had asked for volunteers to go to the leper colony. (Only one priest of the entire Vicariate did not answer his appeal; the rest cheerfully expressed their willingness to take Damien's place, for it was well known that he could not live long, and from their ranks the Bishop had chosen Father Wendelin.) Then, in November, on the dawn of a stormy morning, Mother Marianne and Sisters Vincent McCormick and Leopoldina Burns were disembarked from the "Lehua."

The priest's days, his last days, were suddenly bright by the kindness of strangers. It seemed as though his dreams were coming true. Not only were helpers by his side, but gifts and messages of solicitude began to come from all over the globe and the clouds of his despair rolled away before the realization that the world was at last understanding the needs of the lepers. All the hopes that he had ever entertained now came back as each steamer brought concrete evidences of men's concern. From England an Anglican clergyman, the Rev. H. H. Chapman, sent a cheque for nearly one thousand pounds, the result of a fund contributed by people of all creeds. In Honolulu a banker donated enough money to build a Home* for the girls and young women of the settlement. These generosities were but a few of the many which the colony, after a history of neglect and privation, was suddenly to experience. At the time the money was received from the Rev. Mr. Chapman, Damien had reason to believe that there were a group of bigoted anti-Catholics who were intriguing against him,

* Later known as the Bishop Home, after its kind patron, Mr. C. R. Bishop. And before he died, Damien was to learn that another generous citizen of Honolulu, Mr. H. P. Baldwin, had promised to provide a similar institution for the boys.

and were proposing that the contemplated schools at Molokai should be staffed entirely by Protestant instructors. Indignant at this news the priest told Dutton that he would devote the entirety of the English cheque to Catholic charities. His even tempered assistant objected and, after several hours of argument, convinced him that such an action would be both unjust and unwise.

The new Girls' Home was to be erected at Kalaupapa and, as the Sisters were to be in charge, they took up their residence in that village. Wasting no time, they set to work the day after their arrival, re-enacting the accomplishments of their early days at the Branch Hospital in an orgy of scrubbing and cleaning. With bandages and ointment brought from Honolulu they established a clinic for the dressing of the lepers' sores, and for those unfortunates who could not walk they began a routine of daily visiting, bringing little gifts and washing wounds and ulcers with a feminine gentleness that the invalids had never before known. Once, after attending a dying woman whose condition was particularly repulsive, Sister Leopoldina was moved to ask Mother Marianne, "Mother, what will you do with me if I become a leper?"

"You will never become a leper," was the calm answer. "I know we are all exposed, and I know, too, that God has called us for this work. If we are present, and do our duty, He will protect us. Do not allow it to trouble you, and when the thought comes to you, drive it from your mind." She paused for a moment, then continued with deliberate confidence, "Child, remember, you will never be a leper, nor will any Sister of our Order."

A remarkable statement it was for her to make and certainly one no medical man would have dared to venture. Time has proved she was right. Franciscan Sisters still carry on the heroic work at Molokai but to this day not one of them has ever contracted the awful sickness.

A list of rules, the underlying motive of which was cleanliness, was compiled by Mother Marianne and she required her Sisters should observe them rigorously. Considering conditions, they were as practical precautions as could be devised, although they did not reach the degree of prudence exhibited by a visiting doctor and representative of the Board of Health, of whom the lepers scornfully reported, "When he prepares medicine he puts it on the gate post so we can get it without coming into his yard."

One of the rules was that the Sisters should never partake of a meal with, or that had been cooked by, a diseased person; but there was one time when Sisters Vincent and Leopoldina found they had to break this strict regulation of their Superior's. She had gone a lengthy tour of the settlement with Father Wendelin and Brother Joseph and had given the nuns permission to visit Kalawao village. It was in the nature of a holiday for them, the first time they had set foot outside of Kalaupapa since landing, so busy had they been. Damien had sent his wagon and they rode over the rocky short distance in high spirits. His altar boys met them with offerings of flowers; and the priest, after they had greeted him, despatched them to inspect the church of which he was very proud and which, to attract the natives, was painted in bright colors and extravagantly ornamented. The startled Sisters had never seen anything like it before. Such flamboyant decoration amused them. Discreet smiles were exchanged from the protecting shadows of their habits, and at the first opportunity Sister Leopoldina whispered to her comrade that the exterior reminded her of a *Chinese shop*. This light-hearted moment quickly vanished, however, when, after the church had been suitably seen, they were informed the priest expected them to dine with him and that, in fact, his cook had arranged a special dish in their honor. With mounting gloom, and thinking of Mother Marianne and her rules, they entered the hut and reluctantly sat at the table. Great was their embarrassment and distress, respecting the priest as they did and wishing to please him, yet at the same time realizing, if they did so, they were disobeying their Superior who had so often stressed that under no circumstances were the rules to be broken. The food was brought. Damien, leaning heavily on Brother James (who acted as his nurse) pronounced grace in his hoarse, fading voice, then noticed that his guests made no effort to commence. Timidly they tried to explain, but with his usual strong will he waved aside the objections and insisted they proceed. They obeyed, but with what appetite can be imagined.

The incident shows Damien's characteristic stubbornness, but its sequel reveals what was an equally true trait to him; a readiness to admit a wrong. The very next morning he startled the Sisters by appearing at their house to ask forgiveness. During the night, after reflection, he had seen his mistake and, against the remonstrances and pleas of the Brothers who knew the jolting journey over rough road would afford him intense agony and perhaps have fatal results, he had insisted on being driven to Kalaupapa to express his repentance.

Naturally they were moved by this gesture and when after some rest, for the ride had indeed taxed what little strength remained to him, he was about to return, the Sisters, at a signal from Mother Marianne, knelt beside the wagon. They knew it would be his last visit to Kalaupapa.

"Give us your blessing, Father Damien," said Mother Marianne.

Obediently the trembling, swollen hand was lifted over their bowed heads and the words said. The request pleased him, and as Brother James urged the horse forward, his eyes were wet with tears.

CHAPTER XV

Just before Christmas the weekly steamer brought to Molokai a new friend whose arrival seemed to imbue Damien with a rallying of strength as strange as it was unexpected. The newcomer was Edward Clifford, an English artist, who was to stay two weeks and who had brought from his fellow countrymen several large packing-cases of gifts for the lepers, including a quantity of *gurjum* oil, a product of a certain tree which grows in the Andaman Islands (off the coast of Burma) and which, at that time, many hoped might be the long-sought cure for leprosy.

From the short and sometimes naïve account he left of his journey to the Islands, Mr. Clifford reveals himself as being possessed of precise habits, a discerning eye, and an extremely charitable and pious disposition. This last quality, however, did not prevent him from becoming quite testy at fellow-passengers on the steamer when they interrupted his painting with numerous amiable but foolish questions. Several pages of his book are devoted to such nuisances. He shows further sarcasm at the manners of some Americans, although it seems that his genteel sensibilities were afforded some relief in Boston when he found the inhabitants charming and cultivated in all the social qualities. The tendency of the artist to judge, to a point of fastidiousness, all that he saw by the standards of Mayfair drawing-rooms is not unimportant, in view of the accusations that were to be leveled against Damien (after his death) of being unclean in his personal habits and uncouth in his manner. This Englishman who was so particular in such things, who indeed had refused to come to the island on

193

the same steamer that transported the lepers, and who would not even allow a leper to carry his luggage, this critical and attentive gentleman who was faithfully to record every detail of his visit, saw nothing untoward or wrong with Damien and in fact lived at the priest's house during his stay at the colony.

There was no bond of a common religious persuasion that might have served to shut his eyes to any flaws in the priest's regime; indeed he was a Protestant of the most uncompromising type, viewing all Catholic activities with a dark suspicion. "When I was a little boy (he relates), I thought all Roman Catholics were wicked and went steadily to hell. If I saw a nun I thought she wanted to catch and burn me." The years were to bring a lessening of this sturdy anti-papistry; but, in the same work wherein he praises Damien, the enthusiastic eulogy is solemnly prefaced by a ponderous explanation as to why he objected to Catholicism. This explanation ends with: "So, God helping me, I will never be a Roman Catholic. And having said this, I feel free to tell my story."

His easel was set up in front of the presbytery. There he would sit by the hour and sketch while the priest rested and watched from the shadows of the honeysuckle-covered veranda. The sight of the artist at work was of course great entertainment for the leper children. They used to gather by the score, gravely staring at the miracle of brush and pencil. It was a scene that would have been idyllic if the faces and bodies of the human participants had been but normal, particularly when, to the loud beating of wings, flocks of birds, which the priest had tamed, would descend for their daily quota of crumbs. Occasionally, if Damien's strength permitted, the two men would indulge in polite conversation; a variety of subjects would be discussed, including the differences of their religious beliefs. Clifford was agreeably surprised to find "it was no part of his (Damien's) belief that Protestants must be eternally lost," and it was with the same pleasure that he heard his host speak well of a Protestant native pastor who had come to the colony in charge of his leprous wife. Incidentally this was a relationship quite common at the settlement, which he found hard to understand.

"Would it not be wiser," he asked, "to separate such a pair? Is there not the danger of the healthier one being infected, and thus in time the settlement being burdened with the care of two lepers, instead of one?"

The priest shook his head. "Marital relations do not always mean infection," he explained. "There is a woman in the village who remains healthy, yet she has buried three husbands who have died of the disease and she is now wed to her fourth. I have seen the bad effects of forcible separation of married companions. It gives them an oppression of mind which in many instances is more unbearable than the pains and agonies of the disease itself. Not only is the contented mind of the leper secured by the company of his wife, but he has the enjoyment of good nursing and devoted assistance. As for the children of such a union, they are born clean."

What he said is true. Children born of lepers are free of the disease, although such infants are taken from the parents at an early age as a precaution against any possible contagion.

When Christmas day came, Clifford, who seems to have been able to give a good account of himself in all the pleasant arts, delighted Damien by taking a place in the grim choir whose members another visitor has described as consisting entirely of lepers.

"Several of whom had only two fingers on their hands. The organist had but one hand and even that was maimed; he had fastened, to what remained of his left hand, a stick, and with that he struck the bass notes. Once, in the middle of a piece, I saw a musician lose part of his finger and part of a lip drop off. Several were blind, but it did not matter, for they loved their music . . ."

However, the Englishman, although keeping a good distance from his unfortunate companions, was undaunted, and rendered "Adeste Fideles" in a steady and pleasing voice. After the service he further gladdened his fellow choristers by distributing gifts of coins and trinkets. It was on the Christmas evening he scored his greatest success, for it was then he produced a magic lantern. In the dusk of the tall trees, the lepers thrilled at the visions, almost miraculous to them, of the colored slides. They sat spellbound while he showed them the scenic wonders of distant continents, their first glimpses of cities, and lakes, and icebound fjords. Audiences in the fashionable theaters of great capitals and before the feasts of world-famous celebrities, could not have been more grateful than were that pitiful company.

As a remembrance of his visit to Molokai, Clifford asked his host to write a few words on the fly-leaf of his Bible. In a spidery, shaking hand, for by now he could hardly hold a pen, Damien scrawled: "*I was sick and ye visited me. J. Damien de Veuster.*"

"In London," Clifford told him, "I shall see Cardinal Manning. Would you like to send some word to his Eminence?"

"It is not for such as I to send a message to such a dignitary as he," was the modest reply; then a few moments later: "Although of course I send him my humble respects and thanks."

On the last day of the year Clifford sailed from the settlement. Damien saw to it that the grateful lepers gave the Englishman the same brand of farewell that had been shown the Bishops and the Princess Regent; even insisting on being carried to the landing himself where, leaning on the strong arm of Brother James, he "stood with his people on the rocks till we slowly passed from their sight. The sun was getting low in the heavens, the beams of light were slanting down the mountain sides, and then I saw the last of Molokai in a golden veil of mist."

CHAPTER XVI

His forty-ninth birthday passed and he calmly began to prepare for death.

"I would like to be put by the side of my church," he told his assistants, "under the stout old tree where I rested so many nights before I had any other shelter."

It seemed to be the happiest period of his life, those last few months that were the threshold to his grave. With the certainty that his work would go on, a great tranquillity had come to soothe his restless nature and he was content for the end. He made his will, leaving what few belongings he had to be disposed of at the Bishop's discretion. "How happy I am to have given all to Monseigneur!" he told Father Wendelin. "Now I die poor, having nothing of my own."

To Belgium went the last letter: "Kindly remember me to all the Fathers in Louvain, to Gerard, Leonor and all the family. I am still able, but not without some difficulty, to stand every day at the altar, where I do not forget any of you. Do you, in return, pray and get prayers for me, who am being gently drawn toward the grave. May God strengthen me, and give me the grace of perseverance and of a happy death." And in answer to a solicitous message from Clifford: "I try to make slowly my way of the Cross and hope to be soon on top of my Golgotha."

Until the early part of March he still willed himself to celebrate Mass. Then his body failed completely and he was forced to desist. Even when he was on what was literally his deathbed, he refused to be the conventional invalid. Not for him was there to be the usual air of despair and sorrow that surrounds the doomed; every morning he ordered Brother James and Father Conrady to carry his mattress to the grass patch in front of his house. There every day his lepers, "my people," would come to see him. He permitted no tears and usually had a joke or a kind word for everyone. In the evenings he used to be carried indoors again, and then the shadows outside his door would become crowded with the same friends; their voices would be heard in the gentle chanting that he was so fond of. "It is a pleasant way to die," he said.

Memories occasionally occupied him. He talked of the past, of his early days at the settlement, of the bleak morning on which he had landed. "They are all gone," he said, referring to the lepers who had met him on that day. "And I shall be seeing them soon." Sometimes he talked of Tremeloo; he lived his life over again and wondered whether they remembered him at his first parish.

One morning he extended his hands to Father Wendelin.

"Look at them," he said cheerfully. "All the wounds are healing and the crust is becoming black—that is a sign of death, as you know very well. Look at my eyes. I have seen so many lepers die that I cannot be mistaken. Death is not far off!"

He made a general confession to Wendelin, who then made his to Damien, after which they renewed their vows to their Order. He asked that natives sing his favorite hymn and smiled contentedly when, almost instantly, the sound of their voices was heard. They knew the priest liked the music of their chanting and always a chorus waited patiently outside his house.

"*When, oh when, shall it be given to me*
To behold my God?
How long shall I be captive in this strange land? . . ."

The priest called his assistants to his bedside.

"How good He is," he told them, "to have preserved me long enough to have you by my side to assist me in my last moments, and then to know that the good Sisters of Charity are at the hospital—that is my *Nunc dimittis*. The work of the lepers is assured. I am no longer necessary to them. So before long I shall go up yonder."

"When you are there, Father," asked Wendelin, "you won't forget those whom you are leaving orphans?"

"Oh, no," was the reply. "If I have any credit with God, I shall intercede for all who are in the *leproserie*."

"Leave me your mantle," pleaded the young priest, "that like Elias, I may inherit your great heart."

Even at the moment such hero-worship would not be tolerated by the practical Damien. "What would you do with it?" he asked good-naturedly. "It is full of leprosy."

Near midnight, on the eve of Palm Sunday, he was given Holy Communion for the last time; it was evident he could not survive much longer, and as the news was made known, an anxious, silent crowd gathered around his house to wait in melancholy vigil. Life persisted in him during the entire Sunday. For the most part he was unconscious, although occasionally his eyes would flicker open and he would try to smile at those who watched by his bed. As earthly things slowly receded from his vision, he seemed to see two other figures in the room, one at his head, one at his feet, but he did not say who they were.

Candles were lit that night. In the early hours of the morning he died; the end coming as he had wished it, without a struggle, as though he were falling asleep. In the grayness of the dawn, as Brother Dutton and Father Wendelin tried in vain to hush the tumultuous weeping of the lepers, Brother James told a sad-eyed Mother Marianne that the priest had died peacefully and that "all signs of leprosy had disappeared from the face!" *

* "A remarkable change in his countenance took place before his death, that of the total disappearance of the tubercles with which his face was covered . . ." wrote Brother James in a

They dressed him in his cassock. The Sisters lined his coffin with white silk and covered the outside with black cloth upon which was sewn a white cross. His grave was dug in the cool shadow of the pandanus tree and around it the long line of mourners shuffled in sad and grotesque parade, clad in the pitiful paraphernalia of the burying associations he had founded. Their friend Kamiano was dead but they did not want to accept the mournful fact that he had gone and even when the grave was filled they refused to go. They sat on the ground, beating their breasts, swaying their bodies with misery, after the custom of their ancestors.

"*Au-ee . . .*" went the sad wail. "*Au-ee . . .*"

He was dead, but the bell that tolled his requiem, the bell he had fastened with his own hands on the tiny steeple of St. Philomena's, sent an echo that was to be heard around the world. Damien and Molokai suddenly became familiar names in every country as editors, in an enthusiastic chorus of sympathy and eulogy, spread the news of the priest's death. Religious differences were forgotten. All creeds and those of no creed, united to render common tribute to a man whose courage was beyond the ordinary brands of heroism, for, as the editor of the London *Daily News* wrote:

". . . Almost anyone will risk death in the pursuit of some object he ardently desires; it may be the triumph of a cause, it may be personal renown, or personal advantage, or mere money, or mere pleasure. A brave, ambitious soldier in one of Scott's romances is telling of the glory he hopes to win, and he declares that it would be worth dying for, and then suddenly stops and cries out, 'Dying for?— oh, that's not much—it would be worth living for.' To such a man, to many a man, death on the battlefield would seem nothing to shrink from. But death from the most

letter to Clifford dated three days after Damien died (15th April 1889). Fr. Wendelin also mentions the same phenomenon.

loathsome malady imagination can conceive of, or observation describe—death as the result of a long protracted period of corruption and decay—it calls for the spirit of a martyr to volunteer for a death like that."

The universal pity that had been stirred by the priest's sacrifice did not cease with the newspaper laudations. The world now realized that, while he was gone, other lepers remained, dying and living in the same shameful distress as he had found on Molokai. In India alone it was estimated that there were 250,000 unfortunates, contaminated with the disease, living under appalling conditions, and with their ranks, despite the inroads of death, steadily increasing. In other places it was almost as bad, and there was no doubt that the terror was growing in Africa and China. Individual humanitarians had long been trying to publicize these facts, but it was not until Damien's death that their voices began to be heard; then, with a dramatic suddenness, public opinion was fired and the lethargy of governments was dissipated.

Damien might be dead but his story was not finished, nor is it yet; for his death marked the beginning of a great campaign to stamp out the disease and to make happier the lives of lepers. Following his death, and with it as an inspiration, mass meetings were held in every country, committees were formed, hospitals and doctors endowed. In London, and it is but typical of what was happening in other capitals, the Prince of Wales, later to be King Edward VII, told a distinguished gathering that:

"The heroic life and death of Father Damien has not only roused the sympathy of the United Kingdom, but it has gone deeper—it has brought home to us that the circumstances of our vast Indian and Colonial Empire oblige us, in a measure at least, to follow his example . . ."

With alacrity his listeners (a company of widely disparate interests and beliefs, including the Archbishop of

Canterbury, the Jewish banker Rothschild, the journalist Frank Harris) agreed that the sympathy of England should find expression in a substantial memorial that should take a threefold form: a monument to be erected at Molokai (moved by his friend, Edward Clifford and seconded by the Duke of Westminster); the creation of a Damien Institute where the study of leprosy would be the main feature (moved by Sir James Paget and seconded by Mr. J. Hutchinson); a complete inquiry into the conditions of lepers residing in India and other British possessions, together with a commission to discover steps that should be taken to alleviate, and, if possible, to eradicate the disease (moved by Sir W. Guyer Hunter and seconded by Cardinal Manning).

All three resolutions were to be faithfully carried out. In fulfillment of the first, a British warship carrying a granite cross of beautiful and antique design, was sent to Honolulu that same year. The King of Hawaii accompanied the officers to Molokai and, with the help of Mother Marianne, a site near the Kalaupapa landing was chosen. There it was placed and there today it stands. On its pedestal, for all to see, is a white marble tablet engraved with words particularly appropriate to the memory of Damien:

"Greater love hath no man than this, that a man lay down his life for his friends."

CHAPTER XVII

But amidst all the concordance of praise there was one dissenting note; the pen of the Rev. Charles McEwen Hyde, a Congregational minister living in Honolulu, was at work, answering a colleague in Australia who had written asking for information about the suddenly famous Damien.

LETTER OF REV. C. McE. HYDE

Honolulu, August 2, 1889.

"Rev. H. B. Gage.

"Dear Brother,—In answer to your inquiries about Father Damien, I can only reply that we who knew the man are surprised at the extravagant newspaper laudations, as if he was a most saintly philanthropist. The simple truth is, he was a coarse, dirty man, headstrong and bigoted. He was not sent to Molokai, but went there without orders; did not stay at the leper settlement (before he became one himself), but circulated freely over the whole island (less than half the island is devoted to the lepers), and he came often to Honolulu. He had no hand in the reforms and improvements inaugurated, which were the work of our Board of Health, as occasion required and means provided. He was not a pure man in his relations with women, and the leprosy of which he died should be attributed to his vices and carelessness. Others have done much for the lepers, our own ministers, the government physicians, and so forth, but never with the Catholic idea of meriting eternal life.—Yours, etc.

"C. M. Hyde."

On receipt of this amazing letter, the Rev. Mr. Gage displayed the bad judgment of sending it to the *Sydney Presbyterian* where, unluckily for the clergyman of Honolulu, it was seen by Robert Louis Stevenson.

Unlike Stevenson, Hyde had met Damien. In fact, only four years before the priest's death—this seems to have been unknown to Stevenson—he had written an account of a visit to the leper settlement which was printed in the *Hawaiian Gazette*. In this article he had described Damien as "that noble-hearted Catholic priest who went to Molokai in 1873 to care for the spiritual welfare of those of his faith and whose work has been so successful."

Only four years separated the praise from the slander, and in that brief interval his subject had been a dying and finally a dead man. What then was the reason for the vicious attack, the sudden change of heart? No one was ever to know, nor was the reverend gentleman ever to explain, except to offer proof that Damien was of peasant birth and that such a fact was "presumptive proof that I had equally good reason for saying what else I said in regard to him!"

Stevenson visited Molokai a short time after Damien's death and remained eight days, staying for the most part at Kalaupapa village where he became friends with the Sisters and their charges. His own health was in such a sorry state because of tuberculosis that Mother Marianne was forced to admonish him. "It is not right for you to exert yourself. It may be dangerous in your condition." His only answer was to smile. He persisted in playing games with the leper children, games that would exhaust him until he would be forced to throw himself on the ground and there remain until rested. At such times the good Mother would shake her head. "What could we do," she asked her assistants, "should he have a hemorrhage in this dreadful place where he could not have proper medicine, food or care? He is not thinking of himself, but is determined

204

those children must know how to play before he leaves them!"

While on the island and at Honolulu, Stevenson, who was inclined to be cynical about popular heroes, and who was suspicious of the almost hysterical praise that surrounded the priest, made inquiries about Damien. He frankly records that he was *"suspicious of Catholic testimony"* and avoided, as much as was possible, the prejudices and enthusiasms of any who might be friendly to the priest. He only talked with those *"who had sparred and wrangled with him; who beheld him with no halo . . . Protestants who had opposed the father in his life . . ."* As he did not speak the language of the lepers, those who were his hosts on the Island and those who had made possible his visit to the settlement, probably comprised the majority of this group—an element who had many reasons to dislike the priest. For years Damien had been their bitter opponent and now after his death, as he was suddenly recognized a hero, so they, his antagonists, had become villains. Yet, with some cause perhaps for rancor, they had no great ills to report of Damien.

They readily admitted the major qualities of his worth but grumbled that he was "strongheaded and officious" and that "he had fallen into something of the ways and habits of thought of a Kanaka." There was something of the truth in this last statement. The priest did live like a Hawaiian, that is, he lived in a hut and ate the same fare as his flock, claiming no privileges because of his priestly office or on account of the color of his skin. He worked with his hands in a place where the "white man's prestige" was seeking to be imposed; he was an outsider whose ways were to be deplored. In justification of their own attitude in dealing with the lepers, they made the claim that he was "unpopular with the natives." When, in the comfortable coolness of their starched white duck they scornfully spoke of the priest's "dirty" cassock, they forgot to mention how that dirt had been acquired. If one of those fastidious gentry had but accompanied Damien on what the priest considered a morning's normal work, he would quickly have found his immaculate jacket a different hue.

As to their complaints about his being "ignorant and illiterate" it is doubtful whether many of them had the equal of his education. The triviality and unimportance of this charge has left it, for the main part, unanswered, until it is now quite a popular but erroneous belief. It is true that Damien was no great scholar or reader. The very nature and demands of his work prevented such qualities, but it must be remembered that he could be called a "university man" when such a term was far more uncommon than it is today and that, in addition to his native Flemish, he had a workable knowledge of Latin and Greek and could speak fluently French, English, German and Hawaiian. It is not difficult to understand the psychology of the petulant officials who differed so much in every way from the missionary. As a species they still exist, and one is forever meeting them in distant colonies and tropical ports; pompous individuals, bright with the ties of minor public schools and heavy with the dignity of the government or company they serve.

Stevenson listened to the criticisms and assiduously kept away from the prejudices of "Catholics and friends." On Molokai there was no spoken defense needed for Damien and the author quietly made his own appraisal. He was a keen observer and sometimes the things he saw made him weep. Particularly did he feel for the sufferings of the leper children; and for those who had given their lives to attend them he had an awed admiration.

Before he left the island he gave many gifts to the children, including a piano for the Home. When the Sisters shyly asked him to leave his autograph, he prefaced it with the gentle words of a poem.

To the Reverend Sister Marianne
Matron of the Bishop Home, Kalaupapa

To see the infinite pity of this place,
The mangled limb, the devastated face,
The innocent sufferers smiling at the rod,
A fool were tempted to deny his God.

He sees, and shrinks; but if he look again,
Lo, beauty springing from the breast of pain!
He marks the sisters on the painful shores,
And even a fool is silent and adores.

There was a sterner task awaiting his pen when, the next year, he visited Australia. While in Sydney, somebody attracted his attention to Hyde's letter. Anger would be a mild word to describe the author's reaction. His wife reported that he beat his head and locked himself in a room where he muttered aloud as he wrote. He knew Hyde, and in fact had been a guest at the clergyman's home, but he had also been to Molokai and the words that sprang from the angry writer that day comprise a far greater monument to the leper priest than any structure of stone could possibly be. Contained in the famous document is, however, one error; the author said: "Kalawao, which you have never visited." As has been seen Hyde had been to Molokai and the fact, in view of tribute he wrote at the time, seems to damn him the more.

ROBERT LOUIS STEVENSON'S LETTER*

"*Sydney, February 25, 1890.*

"SIR,

"It may probably occur to you that we have met, and visited, and conversed; on my side, with interest. You may remember that you have done me several courtesies, for which I was prepared to be grateful. But there are duties which come before gratitude, and offences which justly divide friends, far more acquaintances. Your letter to the Reverend H. B. Gage is a document, which, in my sight,

* Reprinted by permission of Chas. Scribner's Sons.

if you had filled me with bread when I was starving, if you had sat up to nurse my father when he lay a-dying, would yet absolve me from the bonds of gratitude. You know enough, doubtless, of the process of canonisation to be aware that, a hundred years after the death of Damien, there will appear a man charged with the painful office of the *devil's advocate*. After that noble brother of mine, and of all frail clay, shall have lain a century at rest, one shall accuse, one defend him. The circumstance is unusual that the devil's advocate should be a volunteer, should be a member of a sect immediately rival, and should make haste to take upon himself his ugly office ere the bones are cold; unusual, and of a taste which I shall leave my readers free to qualify; unusual, and to me inspiring. If I have at all learned the trade of using words to convey truth and to arouse emotion, you have at last furnished me with a subject. For it is in the interest of all mankind and the cause of public decency in every quarter of the world, not only that Damien should be righted, but that you and your letter should be displayed at length, in their true colors, to the public eye.

"To do this properly, I must begin by quoting you at large: I shall then proceed to criticise your utterance from several points of view, divine and human, in the course of which I shall attempt to draw again and with more specification, the character of the dead saint whom it has pleased you to vilify: so much being done, I shall say farewell to you for ever. (See page 203).

"To deal fitly with a letter so extraordinary, I must draw at the outset on my private knowledge of the signatory and his sect. It may offend others; scarcely you, who have been so busy to collect, so bold to publish, gossip on your rivals. And this is perhaps the moment when I may best explain to you the character of what you are to read: I conceive you as a man quite beyond and below the reticences of civility: with what measure you mete, with that shall it be measured you again; with you, at last, I rejoice to feel the button off the foil and to plunge home. And if in aught that I shall say I should offend others, your colleagues, whom I respect and remember with affection, I can but offer them my regret; I am not free, I am inspired by the consideration of interests far more large; and such pain as can be inflicted by anything from me must be indeed trifling when compared with the pain with which they read your letter. It is not the hangman, but the criminal, that brings dishonor on the house.

"You belong, sir, to a sect—I believe my sect, and that in which my ancesters labored—which has enjoyed, and partly failed to utilise, an exceptional advantage in the islands of Hawaii. The first missionaries came; they found the land already self-purged of its old and bloody faith; they were embraced, almost on their arrival, with enthusiasm; what troubles they supported came far more from whites than from Hawaiians; and to these last they stood (in a rough figure) in the shoes of God. This is not the place to enter into the degree or causes of their failure, such as it is. One element alone is pertinent, and must here be plainly dealt with. In the course of their evangelical calling, they—or too many of them—grew rich. It may be news to you that the houses of missionaries are a cause of mocking on the streets of Honolulu. It will at least be news to you, that when I returned your civil visit, the driver of my cab commented on the size, the taste, and the comfort of your home. It would have been news certainly to myself, had any one told me that afternoon that I should live to drag such matter into print. But you see, sir, how you degrade better men to your own level; and it is needful that those who are to judge betwixt you and me, betwixt Damien and the devil's advocate, should understand your letter to have been penned in a house which could raise, and that very justly, the envy and comments of the passers-by. I think (to employ a phrase of yours which I admire) it 'should be attributed' to you that you have never visited the scene of Damien's life and death. If you had, and had recalled it, and looked about your pleasant rooms, even your pen perhaps would have been stayed.

"Your sect (and remember, as far as any sect avows me, it is mine) has not done ill in a worldly sense in the Hawaiian Kingdom. When calamity befell their innocent parishioners, when leprosy descended and took root in the Eight Islands, a *quid pro quo* was to be looked for. To that prosperous mission, and to you as one of its adornments, God had sent at last an opportunity. I know I am touching here upon a nerve acutely sensitive. I know that others of your colleagues look back on the inertia of your church, and the intrusive and decisive heroism of Damien, with something almost to be called remorse. I am sure it is so with yourself; I am persuaded your letter was inspired by a certain envy, not essentially ignoble, and the one human trait to be espied in that performance. You were thinking of the lost chance, the past day; of that which should have been conceived and was not; of the service due and not rendered. *Time was*, said the voice in your ear, in your pleasant room, as you sat raging and writing; and if the words written were base beyond parallel, the rage, I am happy to repeat—it is the only compliment I shall pay you—the rage was almost virtuous. But, sir, when we have failed, and another has succeeded; when we have stood by, and another has stepped in; when we sit and grow bulky in our charming mansions, and a plain, uncouth peasant steps into the battle, under the eyes of God, and succours the afflicted, and consoles the dying, and is himself afflicted in his turn, and dies upon the field of honor—the battle cannot be retrieved as your unhappy irritation has suggested. It is a lost battle, and lost for ever. One thing remained to you in your defeat—some rags of common honor; and these you have made haste to cast away.

"Common honor; not the honor of having done anything right, but the honor of not having done aught conspicuously foul; the honor of the inert: that was what remained to you. We are not all expected to be Damiens;

a man may conceive his duty more narrowly, he may love his comforts better; and none will cast a stone at him for that. But will a gentleman of your reverend profession allow me an example from the fields of gallantry? When two gentlemen compete for the favor of a lady, and the one succeeds and the other is rejected, and (as will sometimes happen) matter damaging to the successful rival's credit reaches the ear of the defeated, it is held by plain men of no pretensions that his mouth is, in the circumstance, almost necessarily closed. Your church and Damien's were in Hawaii upon a rivalry to do well: to help, to edify, to set divine examples. You have (in one huge instance) failed, and Damien succeeded. I marvel it should not have occurred to you that you were doomed to silence; that when you had been outstripped in that high rivalry, and sat inglorious in the midst of your well-being, in your pleasant room—and Damien, crowned with glories and horrors, toiled and rotted in that pig-sty of his under the cliffs of Kalawao—you, the elect who would not, were the last man on earth to collect and propagate gossip on the volunteer who would and did.

"I think I see you—for I try to see you in the flesh as I write these sentences—I think I see you leap at the word pig-sty, a hyperbolical expression at the best. 'He had no hand in the reforms', he was 'a coarse, dirty man'; these were your own words; and you may think it possible that I am come to support you with fresh evidence. In a sense, it is even so. Damien has been too much depicted with a conventional halo and conventional features; so drawn by men who perhaps had not the eye to remark or the pen to express the individual; or who perhaps were only blinded and silenced by generous admiration, such as I partly envy for myself—such as you, if your soul were enlightened, would envy on your bended knees. It is the least defect of such a method of portraiture that it makes the path easy for the devil's advocate, and leaves for the misuse of the slanderer a considerable field of truth. For the truth that is suppressed by friends is the readiest weapon of the enemy. The world, in your despite, may perhaps owe you something, if your letter be the means of substituting once for all a credible likeness for a wax abstraction. For, if that world at all remember you, on the day when Damien of Molokai shall be named Saint, it will be in virtue of one work: your letter to the Reverend H. B. Gage.

"You may ask on what authority I speak. It was my inclement destiny to become acquainted, not with Damien, but with Dr. Hyde. When I visited the lazaretto Damien was already in his resting grave. But such information as I have, I gathered on the spot in conversation with those who knew him well and long; some indeed who revered his memory; *but others who had sparred and wrangled with him,* who beheld him with no halo, who perhaps regarded him with *small respect,* and through whose unprepared and scarcely partial communications the plain, human features of the man shone on me convincingly. These gave me what knowledge I possess; and I learnt it in that scene where it could be most completely and sensitively understood—Kalawao, which you have never visited, about which you have never so much as endeavored to inform yourself: for, brief as your letter is, you have found the means to stumble into that confession. *'Less than one-half* of the island,' you say, 'is devoted to the lepers.' Molokai—'*Molokai ahina'*, the 'grey', lofty and most desolate island—along all its northern side plunges a front of precipice into a sea of unusual profundity. This range of cliff is, from east to west, the true end and frontier of the island. Only in one spot there projects into the ocean a certain triangular and rugged down, grassy, stony, windy, and rising in the midst into a hill with a dead crater: the whole bearing to the cliff that overhangs it somewhat the same relation as a bracket to a wall. With this hint you will now be able to pick out the leper station on a map; you will be able to judge how much of Molokai is thus cut off between the surf and precipice, whether less than a half, or less than a quarter, or a fifth, or a tenth—or say, a twentieth; and the next time you burst into print you will be in a position to share with us the issue of your calculations.

"I imagine you to be one of those persons who talk with cheerfulness of that place which oxen and wainropes could not drag you to behold. You, who do not even know its situation on the n.ap, probably denounce sensational descriptions, stretching your limbs the while in your pleasant parlor on Beretania Street. When I was pulled ashore there one early morning, there sat with me in the boat two Sisters, bidding farewell (in humble imitation of Damien) to the lights and joys of human life. One of these wept silently; I could not withhold myself from joining her. Had you been there, it is my belief that nature would have triumphed even in you; and as the boat drew but a little nearer, and you beheld the stairs crowded with abominable deformations of our common manhood, and saw yourself landing in the midst of such a population as only now and then surrounds us in the horror of a nightmare— what a haggard eye you would have rolled over your reluctant shoulder towards the house on Beretania Street! Had you gone on; had you found every fourth face a blot upon the landscape; had you visited the hospital and seen the butt-ends of human beings lying there almost unrecognisable, but still breathing, still thinking, still remembering; you would have understood that life in the lazaretto is an ordeal from which the nerves of a man's spirit shrink, even as his eye quails under the brightness of the sun; you would have felt it was (even today) a pitiful place to visit and a hell to dwell in. It is not the fear of possible infection. That seems a little thing when compared with the pain, the pity, and the disgust of the visitor's surroundings, and the atmosphere of affliction, disease, and physical disgrace in which he breathes. I do not think I am a man more than usually timid; but I never recall the days and nights I spent upon that island promontory (eight days and seven nights) without heartfelt thankfulness that I am somewhere else. I find in my diary that I speak of my stay as a 'grinding experience': I have once jotted in the margin '*Harrowing* is the word'; and when the Molokii bore me at last towards the outer world, I kept repeating to myself, with a new conception of their pregnancy, those simple words of the song—

" ' 'Tis the most distressful country that ever yet was seen.'And observe: that which I saw and suffered from was a settlement purged, bettered, beautified; the new village built, the hospital and the Bishop Home excellently arranged; the Sisters, the doctor and the missionaries, all indefatigable in their noble tasks. It was a different place when Damien came there, and made his great renunciation, and slept that first night under a tree amidst his rotting brethren: alone with pestilence; and looking forward (with what courage, with what pitiful sinkings of dread, God only knows) to a lifetime of dressing sores and stumps.

"You will say, perhaps, I am too sensitive, that sights as painful abound in cancer hospitals and are confronted daily by doctors and nurses. I have long learned to admire and envy the doctors and nurses. But there is no cancer hospital so large and populous as Kalawao and Kalaupapa; and in such a matter every fresh case, like every inch of length in the pipe of an organ, deepens the note of the impression; for what daunts the onlooker is that monstrous sum of human suffering by which he stands surrounded. Lastly, no doctor or nurse is called upon to enter once for all the doors of that gehenna; they do not say farewell, they need not abandon hope, on its sad threshold; they but go for a time to their high calling, and can look forward as they go to relief, to recreation, and to rest. But Damien shut to with his own hand the doors of his own sepulchre.

"I shall now extract three passages from my dairy at Kalawao.

"A. 'Damien is dead and already somewhat ungratefully remembered in the field of his labors and sufferings. "He was a good man, but very officious," says one. Another tells

214

me he had fallen (as other priests so easily do) into something of the ways and habits of thought of a Kanaka: but he had the wit to recognise the fact, and the good sense to laugh [over] it. A plain man it seems he was; I cannot find he was a popular.'

"B. 'After Ragsdale's death [Ragsdale was a famous Luna, or overseer, of the unruly settlement] there followed a brief term of office by Father Damien which served only to publish the weakness of that noble man. He was rough in his ways, and he had no control. Authority was relaxed; Damien's life was threatened, and he was soon eager to resign.'

"C. 'Of Damien, I begin to have an idea. He seems to have been a man of the peasant class, certainly of the peasant type: shrewd; ignorant and bigoted, yet with an open mind and capable of receiving and digesting a reproof if it were bluntly administered; superbly generous in the least thing as well as in the greatest, and as ready to give his last shirt (although not without human grumbling) as he had been to sacrifice his life; essentially indiscreet and officious, which made him a troublesome colleague; domineering in all his ways, which made him incurably unpopular with the Kanakas, but yet destitute of real authority, so that his boys laughed at him and he must carry out his wishes by the means of bribes. He learned to have a mania for doctoring; and set up the Kanakas against the remedies of his regular rivals; perhaps (if anything matter at all in the treatment of such a disease) the worst thing that he did, and certainly the easiest. The best and worst of the man appear very plainly in his dealings with Mr. Chapman's money; he had originally laid it out [intended to lay it out] entirely for the benefit of Catholics, and even so not wisely, but after a long, plain talk, he admitted his error fully and revised the list. The sad state of the boys' home is in part the result of his lack of control; in part, of his own slovenly ways and false ideas of hygiene. Brother officials used to call it "Damien's Chinatown."

"Well," they would say, "your Chinatown keeps growing." And he would laugh with perfect good nature, and adhere to his errors with perfect obstinacy. So much I have gathered of truth about this plain, noble human brother and father of ours; his imperfections are the traits of his face, by which we know him for our fellow; his martyrdom and his example nothing can lessen or annul; and only a person here on the spot can properly appreciate their greatness.'

"I have set down these private passages, as you perceive, without correction; thanks to you, the public has them in their bluntness. They are almost a list of the man's faults, for it is rather these I was seeking: with his virtues, with the heroic profile of his life, I and the world were already sufficiently acquainted. I was besides a little suspicious of Catholic testimony: in no ill sense, but merely because Damien's admirers and disciples were the least likely to be critical. I know you will be more suspicious still; and the facts set down above were one and all collected from the lips of Protestants who had opposed the father in his life. Yet I am strangely deceived, or they build up the image of a man, with all his weaknesses, essentially heroic, and alive with rugged honesty, generosity and mirth.

"Take it for what it is, rough private jottings of the worst sides of Damien's character, collected from the lips of those who had labored with and (in your own phrase) 'knew the man';—though I question whether Damien would have said that he knew you. Take it, and observe with wonder how well you were served by your gossips, how ill by your intelligence and sympathy; in how many points of fact we are at one, and how widely our appreciations vary. There is something wrong here; either with you or me. It is possible, for instance, that you, who seem to have so many ears in Kalawao, had heard of the affair of Mr. Chapman's money, and were singly struck by Damien's intended wrong-doing. I was struck with that also, and set it fairly down; but I was struck much more by the fact that he had the honesty of mind to be convinced. I may here tell you that it was a long business; that one of his colleagues sat with him late into the night, multiplying arguments and accusations; that the father listened as usual with 'perfect good-nature and perfect obstinacy'; but at the last, when he was persuaded—'Yes,' said he, 'I am very much obliged to you; you have done me a service; it would have been a theft.' There are many (not Catholics merely) who require their heroes and saints to be infallible; to these the story will be painful; not to the true lovers, patrons, and servants of mankind.

"And I take it, this is a type of our division; that you are one of those who have an eye for faults and failures; that you take a pleasure to find and publish them; and that, having found them, you make haste to forget the overvailing virtues and the real success which had alone introduced them to your knowledge. It is a dangerous frame of mind. That you may understand how dangerous, and into what a situation it has already brought you, we will (if you please) go hand-in-hand through the different phrases of your letter, and candidly examine each from the point of view of its truth, its appositeness, and its charity.

"Damien was *coarse*.

"It is very possible. You make us sorry for the lepers who had only a coarse old peasant for their friend and father. But you, who were so refined, why were you not there, to cheer them with the lights of culture? Or may I remind you that we have some reason to doubt if John the Baptist were genteel; and in the case of Peter, on whose career you doubtless dwell approvingly in the pulpit, no doubt at all he was a 'coarse, headstrong' fisherman. Yet even in our Protestant Bibles Peter is called Saint.

"Damien was *dirty*.

"He was. Think of the poor lepers annoyed with this dirty comrade! But the clean Dr. Hyde was at his food in a fine house.

"Damien was *headstrong*.

217

"I believe you are right again; and I thank God for his strong head and heart.

"Damien was *bigoted.*

"I am not fond of bigots myself, because they are not fond of me. But what is meant by bigotry, that we should regard it as a blemish in a priest? Damien believed his own religion with the simplicity of a peasant or a child; as I would I could suppose that you do. For this, I wonder at him some way off; and had that been his only character, should have avoided him in life. But the point of interest in Damien, which has caused him to be so much talked about and made him at last the subject of your pen and mine, was that, in him, his bigotry, his intense and narrow faith, wrought potently for good, and strengthened him to be one of the world's heroes and examplars.

"Damien *was not sent to Molokai, but went there without orders.*

"Is this a misreading? or do you really mean the words for blame? I have heard Christ, in the pulpits of our church, held up for imitation on the ground that His sacrifice was voluntary. Does Dr. Hyde think otherwise?

"Damien *did not stay at the settlement, etc.*

"It is true he was allowed many indulgences. Am I to understand that you blame the father for profiting by these, or the officers for granting them? In either case, it is a mighty Spartan standard to issue from the house on Beretania Street; and I am convinced you will find yourself with few supporters.

"Damien *had no hand in the reforms, etc.*

"I think even you will admit that I have already been frank in my description of the man I am defending; but before I take you up upon this head, I will be franker still, and tell you that perhaps nowhere in the world can a man taste a more pleasurable sense of contrast than when he passes from Damien's 'Chinatown' at Kalawao to the beautiful Bishop-Home at Kalaupapa. At this point, in my desire to make all fair for you, I will break my rule and adduce Catholic testimony. Here is a passage from my dairy about my visit to the Chinatown, from which you will see how it is (even now) regarded by its own officials: 'We went round all the dormitories, refectories, etc.—dark and dingy enough, with a superficial cleanliness, which he [Mr. Dutton, the lay brother] did not seek to defend. "It is almost decent," said he; "the sisters will make that all right when we get them here."' And yet I gathered it was already better since Damien was dead, and far better than when he was there alone and had his own (not always excellent) way. I have now come far enough to meet you on a common ground of fact; and I tell you that, to a mind not prejudiced by jealousy, all the reforms of the lazaretto, and even those which he most vigorously opposed, are properly the work of Damien. They are the evidence of his success; they are what his heroism provoked from the reluctant and the careless. Many were before him in the field; Mr. Meyer, for instance, of whose faithful work we hear too little: there have been many since; and some had more worldly wisdom, though none had more devotion, than our saint. Before his day, even you will confess, they had effected little. It was his part, by one striking act of martyrdom, to direct all men's eyes on that distressful country. At a blow, and with the price of his life, he made the place illustrious and public. And that, if you will consider largely, was the one reform needful; pregnant of all that should succeed. It brought money; it brought (best individual addition of them all) the sisters; it brought supervision, for public opinion and public interest landed with the man at Kalawao. If ever any man brought reforms, and died to bring them, it was he. There is not a clean cup or towel in the Bishop-Home, but dirty Damien washed it.

"Damien *was not a pure man in his relations with women, etc.* How do you know that? Is this the nature of the conversation in that house on Beretania Street which the cabman envied, driving past?—Racy details of the misconduct of the poor peasant priest, toiling under the cliffs of Molokai?

"Many have visited the station before me; they seem not to have heard the rumor. When I was there I heard many shocking tales, for my informants were men speaking with the plainness of the laity; and I heard plenty of complaints of Damien. Why was this never mentioned? and how came it to you in the retirement of your clerical parlor?

"But I must not even seem to decive you. This scandal, when I read it in your letter, was not new to me. I had heard it once before; and I must tell you how. There came to Samoa a man from Honolulu; he, in a public-house on the beach, volunteered the statement that Damien had 'contracted the disease from having connection with the female lepers'; and I find a joy in telling you how the report was welcomed in a public-house. A man sprang to his feet; I am not at liberty to give his name, but from what I heard I doubt if you would care to have him to dinner in Beretania Street. 'You miserable little ———' (here is a word I dare not print, it would so shock your ears). 'You miserable little ———,' he cried, 'if the story were a thousand times true, can't you see you are a million times a lower ——— for daring to repeat it?' I wish it could be told of you that when the report reached you in your house, perhaps after family worship, you had found in your soul enough holy anger to receive it with the same expression: ay, even with that one which I dare not print; it would not need to have been blotted away, like Uncle Toby's oath, by the tears of the recording angel; it would have been counted to you for your brightest righteousness. But you have deliberately chosen the part of the man from Honolulu, and you have played it with improvements of your own. The man from Honolulu—miserable, leering creature —communicated the tale to a rude knot of beachcombing drinkers in a public-house, where (I will so far agree with your temperance opinions) man is not always at his noblest; and the man from Honolulu had himself been drinking—drinking, we may charitably fancy, to excess. It was to your 'dear Brother, the Reverend H. B. Gage,' that you chose to communicate the sickening story; and the blue ribbon which adorns your portly bosom forbids me to allow you the extenuating plea that you were drunk when by you it was done. Your 'dear brother'—a brother indeed—made haste to deliver up your letter (as a means of grace, perhaps) to the religious papers; where, after many months, I have found and read and wondered at it; and whence I have now reproduced it for the wonder of others. And you and your dear brother have, by this cycle of operations, built up a contrast very edifying to examine in detail. The man whom you would not care to have to dinner, on the one side; on the other, the Reverend Dr. Hyde and the Reverend H. B. Gage: the Apia bar-room, the Honolulu manse.

"But I fear you scarce appreciate how you appear to your fellow-men; and to bring it home to you, I will suppose your story to be true. I will suppose—and God forgive me for supposing it—that Damien faltered and stumbled in his narrow path of duty; I will suppose that, in the horror of his isolation, perhaps in the fever of incipient disease, he, who was doing so much more than he had sworn, failed in the letter of his priestly oath—he, who was so much a better man than either you or me, who did what we have never dreamed of daring—he too tasted of our common frailty. 'O, Iago, the pity of it!' The least tender should be moved to tears; the most incredulous to prayer. And all that you could do was to pen your letter to the Reverend H. B. Gage!

"Is it growing at all clear to you what a picture you have drawn of your own heart? I will try yet once again to make it clearer. You had a father: suppose this tale were about him, and some informant brought it to you, proof in hand: I am not making too high an estimate of your emotional nature when I suppose you would regret the circumstance? that you would feel the tale of frailty the more keenly since it shamed the author of your days? and that the last thing you would do would be to publish it in the religious press? Well, the man who tried to do what Damien did, is my father, and the father of the man in the Apia bar, and the father of all who love goodness; and he was your father too, if God had given you grace to see it.

"ROBERT LOUIS STEVENSON"

When Hyde read the letter his only remark was "Stevenson is simply a Bohemian crank, a negligible person, whose opinion is of no value to anyone."

EPILOGUE

Damien was dead. He could not be forgotten. As his generation passed and the years grew, his work became deeper and broader. Forty-six years after the Sisters had so tenderly lined his coffin with their silk, the King of the Belgians was writing to the President of the United States, stating that his subjects were desirous of having the earthly remains of their fellow countryman returned to his native soil. And in Rome, the long and deliberate process, that careful scrutiny with which the Catholic Church examines the lives and accomplishments of those whom their admirers would call "Blessed", had already started.

On January 27th, 1936, the sound of spade and pick could be heard in Kalawao cemetery. There could be heard too the sound of weeping, for they were taking the priest away.

"We have heard your protest and sympathize with your opposition to his removal from your midst" a Bishop, splendid in black canonicals and purple biretta, told the lepers. "But today his native country, which gave him to us, claims him. His country desires to bestow upon him honors which cannot be given in this remote island spot."

They opened the coffin. The lepers filed by to look at what remained of him who had died for lepers. With them were an aged pair who as his "children" had seen the same coffin lowered into the ground. Standing there, among the watchers, were three relatives of Damien, a nun and two priests, Sister Damien Joseph and Fathers Ernest and Cyril. That which they all looked at was finally covered with the scarlet, black and gold Standard of Belgium and was then carried away. The tall trees echoed with the wistful strains of the Island's song of farewell. "Aloha Oe" sang the lepers and some of the older ones shook their heads, for the resting-place of a great man had been disturbed. According to the "taboos" of their ancestors, someone near the corpse would pay forfeit with his life.

In the bright sunshine of Honolulu, khaki-clad gunners bent over silver gleaming breech-blocks. Guns flashed in salute and soldiers stiffened as the body passed. A caisson was his carriage now. As it rumbled along the streets, a colorful throng, the mélange of races that make a Hawaiian crowd, stood still with respect. There was the slow cadence of muffled drums, the subdued commands of officers, and a long procession of white-surpliced priests intoned the *Miserere*. In the Cathedral, the same Cathedral where he had been ordained, clouds of incense eddied as, with all the pomp that he had been so fond of, Pontifical Mass was celebrated before the brilliantly illuminated altar. The sermon ended with: "*Aloha oe, Damien, valiant soldier of Christ, Salvation of Molokai, Honor of Belgium, Glory of the Church, Radiance of God! Aloha oe!*"

Aloha oe! Damien was returning home. Flags dipped and silent crowds stared as the white-hulled steamer stood out from Honolulu harbor. The priest was leaving the Islands. Back at Molokai, while the lepers still grumbled at their loss, the old ones nodded sagely as word came that the captain of the steamer had disappeared from off his own decks while still at sea. They muttered that the forfeit had been paid, the "taboo" had been fulfilled, and indeed no trace of the mariner has ever been found to this day!

Guns thudded again as the ship reached San Francisco. A great city showed that it too could pay tribute to a hero. Once again troops marched and priests sang and crowds stood with bared heads as a gun-carriage rattled to a Cathedral. Once again thuribles swung in a mist of incense through which the yellow flames of the tall candles glowed like haloed stars, once again voices chanted in liturgical magnificence, but this time it was the pallium-draped shoulders of an Archbishop that were bent low, praying for the soul of simple Father Damien.

Under gray skies and in a shroud of pelting rain the ship steered through the Golden Gate and turned south to Panama where amidst all the brilliance of naval ceremonials the flag-covered casket was carried aboard a Belgian man-of-war. Swords flashed, whistles shrilled, and bunting broke in gay salute. Damien would have liked this vessel; she was a fitting craft to carry him who had so enjoyed the glories of spar and canvas. The "Mercator" is a slim-hulled sailing craft, a three-masted barkentine; a training ship of the Belgian navy.

On an Antwerp wharf the King of the Belgians, a slim figure in an unostentatious uniform, stood alongside the scarlet magnificence of the Cardinal Archbishop of Malines. A Prince of the country in which he had been born and a Prince of the church which he had served had come to give greeting to the peasant from Tremeloo.

The work goes on. His dream has come true. Around the world are splendid institutions, staffed by brave and capable men and women. As these last words are written, news comes that another Belgian priest, Fr. L. Lejeune of the Marist Order, after thirty years' work in the Fijian Islands, has contracted the disease. With respect (and awe, too) I salute you, Father Lejeune, and so I am sure does Damien.

FINIS

BIBLIOGRAPHY

A BRIEF HISTORY OF THE HAWAIIAN PEOPLE by *William DeWitt Alexander*. New York, 1891: The American Book Co. 341 pp.

FATHER DAMIEN by *Edward Clifford*. New York, 1890: The Macmillan Co. 179 pp.

FATHER DAMIEN by *Piers Compton*. London, 1933: A. Ouseley, Ltd. 200 pp.

CARE AND TREATMENT OF LEPROUS PERSONS IN HAWAII. House Document No. 470, Seventy-second Congress, Second Session.

UNCLEAN! UNCLEAN! by *Paolo Zappa*. London, 1933: L. Dickson, Ltd. 191 pp.

FATHER DAMIEN by *A. C. Benson and H. F. W. Tatham*. In *Men of Might*, London, 1921: E. Arnold. Also in *The Dove*, Los Angeles, Vol. III, No. 2.

DAMIEN, THE LEPER SAINT by *Irene Caudwell*. London, 1931: P. Allan. 187 pp.

THE SAMARITANS OF MOLOKAI by *Charles Judson Dutton*. New York, 1932: Dodd, Mead & Co. 287 pp.

IN THE SOUTH SEAS by *Robert Louis Stevenson*. New York, 1911: Charles Scribner's Sons. 591 pp.

HISTORY OF THE CATHOLIC MISSION IN THE HAWAIIAN ISLANDS by *Fr. Reginald Yzendoorn*. Honolulu, 1927: Honolulu Star-Bulletin. 254 pp.

FATHER DAMIEN AND THE LEPERS by *Archibald Ballantyne*.

REPORT ON LEPROSY IN THE HAWAIIAN ISLANDS. In *Public Health Reports*, issued by the Supervising Surgeon-General, Marine Hospital Service, Washington, D. C. Vol. XIII, No. 52.

RECOLLECTIONS OF ROBERT LOUIS STEVENSON IN THE PACIFIC *by Arthur Johnstone*. London, 1905: Chatto & Windus. 327 pp.

LIFE AND LETTERS OF FATHER DAMIEN, THE APOSTLE TO THE LEPERS.

MOTHER MARIANNE OF MOLOKAI *by Professor L. V. Jacks*.